C# Core Concepts

How Modern C# Really Works, in Plain English

unQbd

C# Core Concepts: How Modern C# Really Works, in Plain English

Adam Seebeck

Paperback ISBN: 979-8-90377-050-2

unQbd 581 N Park Ave #4201 Apopka, FL 32704 USA

Print Year: 2026

About unQbd

unQbd is a book streaming platform built for modern readers. We publish practical, hands-on books across technical, fiction, and children's categories and make them available to stream from any device for one simple price: $9.99/year.

This book is part of our technical programming series. As a subscriber, you get unlimited access to the full catalog including every title in the series.

Start a free 7-day trial at unqbd.com/app.

About This Book

Who this book is for

This book speaks to developers who already write C# and now want to know what the compiler and runtime actually do. If you have one to three years of professional or hobby experience, or you have completed a solid fundamentals course, you have enough context to follow the reasoning. The text is written for reading or listening away from a screen, so you can absorb the mental models while commuting, exercising, or resting. No second monitor is required; the explanations live in the prose.

What you will learn and build

You will build accurate mental models of how C# 14 on .NET 10 executes your programs. Instead of memorizing syntax, you will learn to trace a promise from the language specification through Roslyn compilation to Intermediate Language, then through the Common Language Runtime to native code. You will learn how value and reference semantics differ, how the generational garbage collector manages object lifetime, how generics avoid boxing while preserving type safety, how closures carry captured variables, how LINQ defers execution through expression trees, how async and await use state machines and continuations, and how nullability, collections, and spans interact with memory safety and performance. The book uses analogies and narrated walkthroughs rather than exhaustive API listings. You will not build a sample application; you will build judgment.

How to use this book (recommended reading path)

Read the four parts in sequence. Part I establishes the habit of runtime thinking. Part II anchors memory and meaning with values, references, and garbage collection. Part III puts abstractions in motion with generics, delegates, LINQ, and async. Part IV applies that foundation to failure design, nullability patterns, and performance instincts. Later chapters assume you have absorbed the earlier mental models, so skipping ahead may leave gaps.

Each chapter closes with a concise recap you can use to test your recall before moving on.

High-level prerequisites

You should already know how to write methods, classes, conditionals, and loops in C#. You do not need a computer science degree, advanced mathematics, or prior knowledge of compilers. The book explains Intermediate Language, just-in-time compilation, and garbage collection from the ground up using plain language and concrete analogies. Familiarity with Visual Studio or the .NET command line is helpful but not required.

Table of Contents

Part I: Starting Map

Chapter 1: Thinking Like the Runtime

What You Will Learn

- Understand the three-layer reasoning habit of tracing behavior from language promise through compiler output to runtime execution
- Recognize the four roles in the modern .NET 10 toolchain and how handoffs work between them
- Distinguish between what the C# language guarantees, what Roslyn emits, and what the Common Language Runtime does
- Explain why this book treats C# 14 as a clarifying lens rather than a feature catalog
- Trace unexpected behavior back through source intent, Intermediate Language, and execution

Prerequisites

> *No additional prerequisites beyond those listed in About This Book.*

Why This Matters

Developers who write C# every day often treat the language as a black box. When a program surprises them, they guess. They blame the compiler, or they blame the runtime, or they rewrite perfectly good source code without knowing which layer actually failed them. This habit wastes hours and teaches nothing.

You already know how to write C#. What you need now is the ability to predict what will happen before you run the program, and to diagnose what did happen when your prediction fails. It's not enough to trust the black box; you need to know which layer actually failed you.

This chapter gives you that map. Everything that follows, from memory management to asynchronous execution, depends on this three-layer habit.

Core Analogy

Imagine an architect sketching a welcoming front porch with exact dimensions. A drafter then redraws that sketch into a universal construction specification that does not depend on any local building code. That specification travels to a job site far away, where a construction crew reads it and builds the porch using local lumber and tools. When the finished porch sags, the foreman checks the original sketch, the translated spec, and the on-site workmanship before deciding where the fault lies.

In this analogy, the architect's sketch is your C# source code stating clear intent. The drafter is the Roslyn compiler, translating that intent into Intermediate Language stored inside an assembly. The universal specification is the assembly itself, which travels to any compatible machine that carries the .NET 10 runtime and its dependencies. The drafting office and tool shed that equip both the drafter and the crew map to the free and open-source .NET 10 Software Development Kit; it provides the tools, yet it remains distinct from the hands that build. The construction crew is the Common Language Runtime, reading that specification and adapting it to the actual processor. The sagging porch is any unexpected behavior; the foreman's inspection is your disciplined trace back through language promise, compiler output, and runtime execution.

Mental Model

The modern .NET toolchain contains four distinct roles. The free and open-source .NET 10 Software Development Kit (SDK) provides the toolset. Roslyn, the C# compiler, transforms your source into Intermediate Language. The assembly is the portable container that carries that Intermediate Language. The Common Language Runtime is the execution engine that brings it to life on a specific chip.

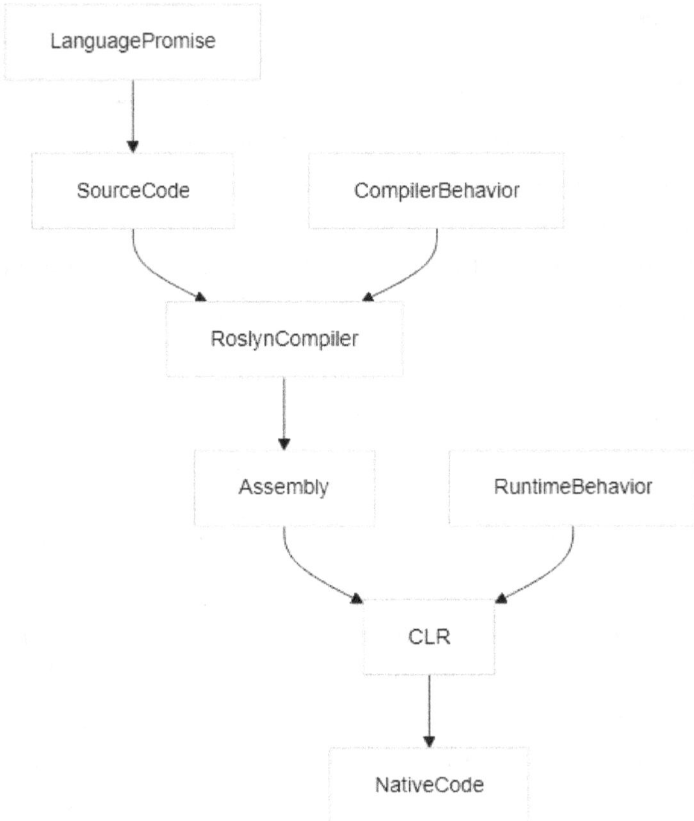

Your job as a developer is to reason across three layers mapped to those four roles. The top layer is the language promise living in your source code. C# 14, which reached general availability in November 2025, defines those guarantees. The middle layer is compiler behavior; Roslyn decides how to express your intent in Intermediate Language. The bottom layer is runtime behavior. The Common Language Runtime translates Intermediate Language into native machine code, meaning the actual instructions understood by the specific processor in front of you; that translation step is just-in-time compilation itself, and through tiered compilation the runtime keeps re-optimizing hot paths as the program runs. Alongside that, it provides managed execution, memory management, and thread pool services.

When you read C# source, you are reading the architect's vision. When you build, Roslyn produces the specification. When you run, the Common Language Runtime builds the porch. A mismatch can appear at any handoff, though in daily practice the source layer is where most errors begin. The language spec might be misunderstood. The Just-In-Time compiler, which is part of the runtime, might optimize away a branch you expected to remain when it turns Intermediate Language into native code. The runtime might reorder instructions within the limits of the .NET memory model and observable behavior rules; those constraints protect single-threaded logic, but the result can still surprise you if you expected a literal step-by-step match to the source.

Treat the source code as a question, not an answer.

This book uses C# 14 as a clarifying lens, not a feature catalog. Where a new C# 14 capability helps explain what the compiler or runtime is doing, we will mention it. We will not tour every new keyword for its own sake. The runtime mechanics have stayed stable across versions; most new syntax compiles down to patterns the runtime already understood before that syntax existed.

New syntax is not new machinery.

During a migration last year, I traced a phantom bug to a stale assembly in the deployment folder; the team had nearly rewritten the caching layer before we checked the handoff between build and runtime. That is why you trace before you blame.

.NET 10 is a Long-Term Support (LTS) release, supported through November 2028. The concepts here are evergreen, but we will note version callouts when a capability changed recently.

Walkthrough

You sketch a welcoming front porch. You want a deck ten feet wide, six feet deep, with a roof pitched at thirty degrees. This is your source code; it states intent in terms humans understand.

You hand the sketch to a drafter. She does not build anything. Instead, she redraws your vision into a universal specification that uses no brand names and assumes no local lumber yard. Every joint, angle, and beam is described precisely, but in a language any qualified crew can read. This is Roslyn compiling your C# into Intermediate Language and sealing it inside an assembly. The assembly is just a file, but it is a file that can travel to any supported operating system where the .NET 10 runtime and compatible dependencies are present.

That specification arrives at a job site two thousand miles away. The local crew cannot read your original sketch. They read the universal spec. They choose local pine because that is what grows nearby. They use their own saws and their own nails. The finished porch looks exactly like your sketch, but it is built from local materials. This is the Common Language Runtime executing your Intermediate Language on an actual processor. The chip might be from Intel, AMD, or Arm; the runtime adapts the spec to whatever is available.

Six months later, the porch sags three inches on the left. The homeowner calls you. You do not immediately blame the pine, nor do you blame the architect's pencil. You inspect the original sketch first. It specified a support post every four feet. You inspect the drafter's universal spec next. It preserved that spacing.

Finally, you inspect the workmanship and the local conditions. The crew built exactly what the spec described; the spec preserved exactly what the sketch described; and the sketch itself called for nails where the load needed bolts, so every layer faithfully delivered the wrong fastener. The soil was also wetter than the standard assumed. The fastener fault traces all the way back to the source; the wet soil is the runtime layer, where the execution environment diverged from the plan.

Now reverse the scenario. You inspect the drafter's universal spec and discover that your thirty-degree roof pitch was translated into a different angle. The crew built faithfully from that spec. The fault lies at the compiler layer, where Roslyn translated your intent into Intermediate Language in a way you did not expect. Or perhaps the crew built from an old spec left in the truck; you find this only because you compared the sketch to the actual assembly they used. Either way, the mismatch is caught by inspecting the specification itself.

Consider a third case. The sketch forgot to mention footings entirely. The drafter and the crew both did exactly what the drawing asked. The fault lies in the source code itself; the author omitted a requirement.

Finally, imagine the sketch included a note that you thought guaranteed automatic footings, but the C# language specification offers no such promise. The drafter and crew followed the real rules, not your assumption. The fault lies in your understanding of the language promise, not in the specification, which is the contract they both followed.

This is how you think like the runtime. You separate the three layers and you inspect the handoffs.

Story or Scenario

Last autumn, Maya's team migrated a pricing service to .NET 10. One morning, she noticed that an early-exit condition appeared to skip valid customers. Her teammate immediately suspected the Common Language Runtime. He claimed the new runtime was mishandling true and false values. Maya paused.

She checked the source first. The language promises that a compound condition stops evaluating as soon as the answer is known, and the source looked correct. Then she conceptually traced the compiled output; in practice, directly reading Intermediate Language is an advanced step, but she verified that Roslyn had compiled the method faithfully and the decision points in the intermediate specification were exactly where she expected.

Finally, she checked the deployment. The server was running an older assembly from an old build folder. The runtime was executing last week's logic against this week's database schema. The runtime was innocent; the handoff between build and deployment had failed. Maya's team fixed their pipeline and added build-label verification. From that day on, they traced every surprise through source, compiler, and runtime before assigning blame.

Common Misconceptions

- **"The compiler and the runtime are the same thing."** Both tools ship with the free .NET 10 Software Development Kit, so it is easy to treat them as one invisible step. They are not. The SDK is the toolbox that contains the compiler, the runtime, and many other utilities; the runtime is specifically the execution engine. Roslyn produces Intermediate Language; the Common Language Runtime consumes it and turns it into native code. Treat them as separate handoffs.
- **"If the program behaves strangely, the language specification is probably wrong."** We trust our own source code, so blaming the contract feels natural. Do not confuse a faulty understanding with a faulty specification. The C# language specification is the contract; it is not a suspect. Strange behavior almost always means you are

misunderstanding what the compiler emitted or how the runtime executed it. Audit your own understanding before you doubt the contract.

- **"C# 14 features change how the runtime fundamentally works."** New syntax feels like new magic underneath, but that feeling is misleading. Most C# 14 capabilities are conveniences that Roslyn translates into Intermediate Language patterns the runtime already understands. The runtime mechanics remain stable. Do not assume a new keyword requires new runtime support.
- **"Intermediate Language is just another text format like source code."** The word language in the name invites this confusion. Intermediate Language is a binary instruction set for a virtual machine. The assembly is a portable executable container, not a text file you read like C# source.

Summary

Thinking like the runtime means tracing every behavior through three layers. Your C# source is the architect's sketch, stating intent. Roslyn is the drafter, turning that intent into portable Intermediate Language inside an assembly. The Common Language Runtime is the construction crew, adapting that specification to the local processor. When the porch sags, you inspect the sketch, the spec, and the workmanship in that order. This habit separates language promises from compiler choices from runtime realities, and it is the foundation for every chapter that follows.

Key Terms

- **Intermediate Language (IL):** The binary instruction set that Roslyn produces from your C# source. It serves as a compact, platform-neutral representation that the Common Language Runtime translates into native machine code during execution.
- **Roslyn:** The free and open-source C# compiler that transforms your source code into Intermediate Language and packages it inside an assembly.

- **Common Language Runtime (CLR):** The execution engine that reads Intermediate Language from an assembly and translates it into native machine code for the specific processor where the program runs.
- **Native machine code:** The processor-specific instructions that the Common Language Runtime generates from Intermediate Language so the physical chip can actually execute your program.
- **Assembly:** The portable container that carries Intermediate Language. It can run on any machine with a compatible .NET runtime, a supported operating system, and the dependencies it expects.
- **.NET 10 Software Development Kit (SDK):** The free and open-source build-time toolset that includes the compiler, project build tools, and a copy of the runtime for local development. Don't confuse it with the execution runtime itself: build tools and execution engine are different jobs, and a server with the wrong one installed cannot run your service.
- **Language promise:** The guarantee made by the C# language specification about how a given construct must behave. This is the top layer of the three-layer reasoning habit.
- **Compiler behavior:** The specific choices Roslyn makes when turning your source intent into Intermediate Language. This is the middle layer of the three-layer reasoning habit.
- **Runtime behavior:** The actions the Common Language Runtime takes when translating Intermediate Language into native machine code and managing execution on the actual chip. This is the bottom layer of the three-layer reasoning habit.

Mini Quiz

1. **In the porch analogy, which layer represents the universal construction specification that travels to the job site?**

   A. The C# source code

   B. The Intermediate Language inside the assembly

   C. The Common Language Runtime

   D. The native machine code

2. **In the core analogy, what does the architect's original sketch represent?**

   A. The C# source code

   B. The Intermediate Language inside the assembly

   C. The Common Language Runtime

   D. The native machine code

3. **Which role in the toolchain translates Intermediate Language into native machine code and manages execution?**

   A. Roslyn

   B. The assembly

   C. The Common Language Runtime

   D. The .NET 10 SDK

4. **What is Roslyn's primary responsibility?**

   A. Executing native machine code on the processor

   B. Translating C# source into Intermediate Language

   C. Managing memory and threads during program execution

   D. Deploying assemblies to the target server

5. **Which of the following best describes an assembly?**

   A. A text file containing C# source code

   B. A runtime process that manages memory

   C. A local build of native machine code for one processor

   D. A portable container that carries Intermediate Language

6. **In Maya's story from this chapter, what was the actual cause of the pricing service bug?**

A. Roslyn compiled the boolean logic incorrectly

B. The Common Language Runtime mishandled short-circuit evaluation

C. The server was running an older assembly from a stale build folder

D. The C# language specification changed between versions

Answers are provided in the Answer Key at the end of the book.

Reflection Prompts

- Recall the last time a program surprised you. Did you blame the compiler, the runtime, or your own code first? How would the three-layer habit have changed your first move?
- Describe a recent handoff between tools in your daily workflow. Where is the weakest link between your source intent and what actually executes?
- Identify one C# feature you previously thought changed runtime behavior. After reading this chapter, does it seem more likely to be compiler sugar or a genuine runtime change?

Chapter 2: From Source to Running Program

What You Will Learn

- Understand how C# source becomes Intermediate Language inside an assembly
- Recognize the usual Common Language Runtime path, where Intermediate Language is translated during execution
- Distinguish just-in-time compilation, which delays translation until needed, from NativeAOT, which moves native translation earlier
- Explain why first execution can include translation cost as well as program cost
- Reason about tiered just-in-time compilation as a warm-up process for frequently used methods and paths
- Understand how dynamic profile-guided optimization uses real execution behavior to improve hot paths

Prerequisites

- Familiarity with the Chapter 1 habit of reasoning through language promise, compiler behavior, and runtime behavior
- The roles of the .NET 10 Software Development Kit, Roslyn, assemblies, Intermediate Language, and the Common Language Runtime
- The idea from Chapter 1 that source code expresses intent, while execution depends on what the compiler and runtime actually produce
- The Chapter 1 architect, drafter, and local crew analogy as background for understanding handoffs

Why This Matters

Many C# developers think compiling a program means turning source directly into final instructions for the processor. That model is wrong for normal .NET execution. Roslyn prepares Intermediate Language inside an assembly. The Common Language Runtime translates that Intermediate Language into native machine code later, while the program runs.

That timing changes how you interpret behavior. The first time a method runs, the runtime may pay a translation cost. Later, if the method becomes popular, the runtime can replace the first translation with a better one. Your program is not frozen at build time. It adapts.

Treat first-run timings as suspect.

This execution map matters before later chapters discuss memory, generics, delegates, Language Integrated Query, and async. Those topics all sit on the same foundation: C# source begins the journey, but the running program emerges through compiler and runtime handoffs.

Core Analogy

Chapter 1 used a construction model: an architect sketches, a drafter prepares a universal specification, and a local crew builds with local materials. This chapter keeps that handoff idea but changes the lens. Now you are watching a translator work with a document.

Your C# source is the original document, written for human developers. Roslyn is the first translator in the chain, but it does not translate the document into one local spoken language. It prepares a neutral draft that many local translators can understand. That neutral draft is Intermediate Language, carried inside an assembly.

When the program runs, the Common Language Runtime becomes the local translator. It reads the neutral draft and translates needed passages into the language of the local machine, which means native machine code for the current processor.

A passage in this analogy is a method. A route is a frequently traveled way through one or more passages, including branches and calls into other methods. Hot code is the route the program keeps asking for.

The translator does not polish the whole book before anyone can read page one. The translator gives a quick rough translation for a passage when someone first asks for it. If people keep rereading the same passage, the translator returns to it and produces a more polished local version. That is tiered just-in-time compilation, guided by dynamic profile-guided optimization.

The mapping is direct. Source is the original document. Intermediate Language is the neutral draft. The assembly is the folder carrying that draft. The Common Language Runtime is the local translator. Native machine code is the local-language version the machine can actually read. Methods are passages. Hot paths are the routes readers keep taking through those passages.

Source is not the final product.

Mental Model

Normal C# and .NET execution follows the usual Common Language Runtime path. Roslyn compiles source into Intermediate Language inside an assembly, and the runtime translates that Intermediate Language into native machine code during execution. Use this model unless you know a program was built with a different deployment approach such as NativeAOT.

Keep the hierarchy clear. A program contains methods. A method contains possible paths. A path is the route execution takes through branches and calls. A branch chooses one direction inside a method. A call enters another method. Hot code is code the runtime observes being used frequently. A hot path is a frequently traveled route through methods, branches, and calls.

The processor cannot run Intermediate Language directly. When execution is about to enter a method and no native code is ready for that method, the runtime asks the just-in-time compiler to translate it. Just-in-time compilation, often called JIT compilation, means translation happens when the program needs the method, not when the assembly is first loaded.

The runtime stores that native translation for reuse. Later entries into the same method do not need to pay the same first translation cost again, unless the runtime replaces the translation with a better one.

Tiered just-in-time compilation adds a second step. The first native translation is fast to produce. It is good enough to start running. Later, if the runtime observes that a method or path is used frequently, it treats that code as hot. The runtime can then compile a more optimized version and use that version going forward.

Dynamic profile-guided optimization, often shortened to dynamic PGO, supplies the evidence. The runtime observes real behavior while the program runs. It learns which branches are common, which concrete types actually appear behind interface or virtual calls, and which calls deserve more attention. Those facts matter because a call that usually reaches the same target is easier to streamline, and a branch that usually goes one way lets the native translation favor the common route.

Do not benchmark the translator by accident.

Warm-up matters because the first execution of a method can include the cost of translation. Later executions can reuse native code, and hot paths can receive better native code. A quick measurement taken at startup often measures the translator and the program together.

During a Windows worker service startup investigation, I separated the first job from the tenth before comparing formatter time, because the first job included runtime translation work. The first job ran noticeably slower, and from the second job on, the times settled.

NativeAOT is the contrast in translation timing. Source still goes through the normal front end into Intermediate Language assemblies, then NativeAOT uses those assemblies to produce a native executable or other ahead-of-time output before the program runs. The motivation is to move native translation earlier, often to change startup, deployment, or runtime tradeoffs. That does not make it automatically better for every program. It changes when the bill is paid.

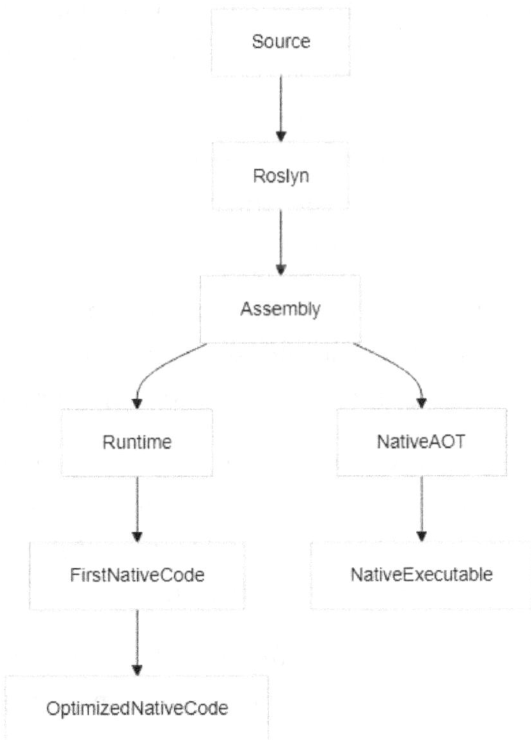

One limit of the translator analogy matters. A human translator may change meaning by accident. The

Common Language Runtime is not allowed to change the language promise. The optimized native code must preserve the behavior promised by C# and represented by the assembly. The runtime can change how work is performed, not what the program means.

Walkthrough

You begin with a small C# program. Think of it as the original document. It is written for people first: you, your teammates, code reviewers, and future maintainers. The language rules say what the program means, but the text itself is not what the processor will execute.

Roslyn reads that source and prepares the neutral draft: Intermediate Language inside an assembly. At this point, you do not yet have the final local translation. You have a portable representation that can travel to supported machines with a compatible .NET runtime, the expected operating system support, and the dependencies the program needs.

Now the program starts on the normal just-in-time path. The Common Language Runtime opens the assembly and begins reading the neutral draft. It does not translate every method at once. The runtime waits until execution is about to enter a method and no native code is ready for that method.

The just-in-time compiler then translates that method into native machine code for the current processor. This is the quick rough translation in the chapter analogy. The runtime stores the translated native code so later entries into the same method can reuse it.

That first translation still must be correct. Rough does not mean sloppy. It means the runtime chooses a translation strategy that is fast to produce and good enough for early execution. The language promise remains intact.

The program keeps running. Most methods are touched once or only a few times. Those passages do not deserve a polished rewrite. Spending extra time optimizing cold code would be wasteful, because the program would pay for polish that almost nobody reads.

One route behaves differently. Suppose a request handler enters a parsing method, follows the same validation branch most of the time, and calls the same calculation method again and again. The runtime sees the repeated use. That route through methods, branches, and calls is a hot path.

Tiered just-in-time compilation now matters. The runtime can replace the first native translation with a more optimized native translation. Dynamic profile-guided optimization helps decide what the polished translation should favor, because the runtime has been watching real behavior rather than guessing from the page.

For example, the runtime may learn that a call usually reaches the same concrete method, or that a branch usually goes one direction. Those observations can help the runtime produce native code that fits the actual workload. The result is not a different program. It is a better local translation of the same program.

This is why a long-running service can feel different from a tiny console experiment. The service gives the runtime time to observe, classify, and improve hot passages. The tiny experiment may finish before the translator has any reason to polish anything.

Measure warm and cold separately.

Now compare that with NativeAOT. In the NativeAOT route, the source still goes through compilation into Intermediate Language assemblies, but native output is prepared ahead of execution. The program starts with native code already produced. This chapter is not deployment advice. The execution contrast is the point: just-in-time compilation translates when needed during execution, while NativeAOT moves native translation before execution begins.

The practical instinct is clear. When you reason about normal .NET execution, picture an adaptive translator. The first version gets you moving. The later version favors passages the program proves it cares about. If you time the first read of a passage, you are timing translation as well as reading.

Story or Scenario

I once watched a team investigate an internal reporting service where the first report after startup took longer than the next ten. The first reaction in the chat was familiar: something must be wrong with the report logic.

They controlled the obvious confounders before blaming the code. They ran the same report parameters each time, warmed the database connection, checked that the query duration stayed steady, and confirmed that the same formatting routine ran on every report request. The database time did not explain the drop. The formatting time did.

A senior developer reframed the problem using the translator model. The source became Intermediate Language at build time, but the native version of the hot formatting path was created as the service ran. The first request paid for rough translation. Repeated requests made the path hot. Tiered just-in-time compilation and dynamic profile-guided optimization then gave the service a better local translation.

The team changed its measurement habit. Startup measurements stayed separate from warmed-up measurements. They still cared about the first request, but they no longer confused it with steady-state behavior. The takeaway was practical: before blaming your source, ask whether you are watching the translator at work.

Common Misconceptions

- Compiling C# source produces the final processor instructions. This belief is tempting because many tools use the word compile as if it always means final machine code. Normal .NET compilation produces Intermediate Language in an assembly, and the Common Language Runtime produces native machine code later. Avoid the mistake by separating Roslyn's build-time work from the runtime's execution-time work.
- Intermediate Language is slow because it is not native machine code. This belief comes from treating Intermediate Language as if the processor interprets it line by line. The processor runs native machine code produced by the runtime. Keep the model clear: Intermediate Language is the neutral draft, and native machine code is the local translation.
- Just-in-time compilation means the whole application is compiled when it starts. This is wrong because methods are translated when execution needs them. Startup does not automatically pay for every

possible path. Reason about the methods that actually run, especially during first use.

- The first timing result is the cleanest result. This is a common testing mistake because the first number feels untouched. In normal .NET execution, the first run can include just-in-time compilation and other warm-up effects. Treat first-run timings as a separate category, not as steady-state truth.
- Optimized hot code has different meaning from the original source. This fear is understandable because the runtime changes the native translation over time. The corrected model is that optimization changes the manner of execution, not the destination. The language promise and the assembly's meaning still control the allowed behavior.
- NativeAOT is just a faster version of just-in-time compilation. This is too vague to be useful. NativeAOT moves native compilation ahead of execution, while just-in-time compilation performs translation during execution as needed. Distinguish the timing of translation before comparing tradeoffs.

Summary

A C# program normally travels from source to Intermediate Language, then from Intermediate Language to native machine code while it runs. Roslyn prepares the neutral draft inside an assembly. The Common Language Runtime acts as the local translator, producing native code for the current machine.

Modern .NET execution is adaptive. Tiered just-in-time compilation starts with a quick translation, stores it for reuse, then improves hot passages with help from dynamic profile-guided optimization. NativeAOT is the ahead-of-time contrast, where native translation happens before the run. Keep the translator model in mind: when a program first starts, you may be watching both the program and its translator.

Key Terms

- Normal C# and .NET execution: The usual path where Roslyn compiles C# source into Intermediate Language inside an assembly, then the

Common Language Runtime just-in-time compiles that Intermediate Language during execution.

- Just-in-time compilation: The runtime translation of Intermediate Language into native machine code when execution is about to enter a method and no native code is ready yet. The runtime stores that translated native code so later entries can reuse it.
- Tiered just-in-time compilation: The runtime strategy of producing a quick first translation, then replacing frequently used methods or execution routes with more optimized translations after observing real execution.
- Dynamic profile-guided optimization: Runtime optimization guided by information collected while the program runs. Observations about common branches, actual types, and frequent call targets help the runtime generate better native code for hot code.
- Hot path: A frequently traveled execution route through methods, calls, and branches. In the chapter analogy, it is the passage, or route through passages, everyone keeps rereading.
- Cold code: Code that runs rarely or only once. The runtime avoids spending unnecessary polishing effort on it because the payoff is low.
- NativeAOT: The ahead-of-time compilation option that works after source has been compiled into Intermediate Language assemblies, then produces a native executable or other ahead-of-time output before the program runs. It changes when translation happens, not the meaning promised by C#.
- Warm-up: The early execution period when the runtime may still be translating methods and learning which paths are hot. First-run measurements include warm-up costs, so they are not the same as steady-state measurements.

Mini Quiz

1. **In normal C# and .NET execution, what does Roslyn produce from C# source?**

   A. Final processor instructions for every supported machine

   B. Intermediate Language inside an assembly

   C. A NativeAOT executable every time

   D. A runtime profile of hot paths

2. **In the normal just-in-time path, what happens when execution is about to enter a method and no native code is ready?**

   A. The Common Language Runtime translates that method into native machine code

   B. Roslyn recompiles the entire project from source

   C. NativeAOT replaces the assembly with a new executable

   D. The processor runs Intermediate Language directly

3. **After the Common Language Runtime translates a method into native machine code, what happens on later entries to that method?**

   A. The runtime can reuse the translated native code

   B. Roslyn must rebuild the assembly each time

   C. The method becomes source code again

   D. The processor switches to interpreting comments

4. **A reporting service runs the same formatting routine on every report request. The team verifies that database time, network latency, and input size stayed stable, yet later requests run faster than the first few. Which explanation best fits this chapter's model?**

   A. The source code changed after the first request

   B. Intermediate Language became less portable over time

   C. The runtime may have translated and later optimized a hot path

   D. NativeAOT must have been enabled automatically

5. **What does dynamic profile-guided optimization use to guide better native code generation?**

   A. Variable names and comments from the source file

   B. Real behavior observed while the program runs, such as common branches and call targets

   C. The number of assemblies in the application

   D. The date when the project was created

6. **Which statement about NativeAOT is correct?**

   A. It means the processor interprets Intermediate Language faster

   B. It changes the meaning promised by the C# language

   C. It is the same thing as tiered just-in-time compilation

   D. It moves native compilation ahead of program execution after the Intermediate Language assembly stage

Answers are provided in the Answer Key at the end of the book.

Reflection Prompts

- Describe a time when the first run of a program behaved differently from later runs.
- Identify one method, routine, or request path in an application you know that likely becomes hot.
- Compare normal just-in-time execution and NativeAOT in terms of when translation happens.
- Recall a performance measurement you trusted. Decide whether it measured warm-up, steady state, or both.

Part II: Memory and Meaning

Chapter 3: Values, References, Copies, and Text

What You Will Learn

- Tell when an assignment makes an independent copy
- Tell when an assignment shares access to the same object
- Predict why changing one copied struct does not change the original
- Predict why changing one shared object is visible through another variable
- Reason about arrays as shared objects, even when their elements are values
- Explain why strings are shared objects that cannot be edited in place
- Explain boxing as a copied value wrapped so it can be treated like an object

Prerequisites

- Familiarity with the three-layer reasoning habit from Chapter 1: language promise, compiler behavior, and runtime behavior
- The idea from Chapter 2 that source syntax is not the same thing as runtime behavior

Why This Matters

Many C# bugs are not caused by syntax. They come from a wrong guess about sharing. You assign one variable to another, pass a value into a method, change a property, append text, or hand a value to an API that expects something object-like. The program compiles. The surprise appears later, when one value changed and another did not, or when two names turned out to be looking at the same object all along.

This chapter gives you the most useful dividing line in day-to-day C#: value semantics versus reference semantics. If you can predict whether an operation makes an independent copy or shares access to one underlying object, many confusing behaviors become ordinary. Later in the chapter, that object-like handoff gets a name: boxing.

Don't debug from folklore.

The right rule is not "structs are on the stack" and "classes are on the heap." That rule is tempting because it points your attention at storage instead of meaning. C# first promises how values behave. The runtime then chooses where and how to store them while preserving that promise.

Core Analogy

A value assignment is like handing someone a photocopy. The other person gets their own sheet of paper. If they write on it, your sheet does not change.

A reference assignment is like giving two people the same shared online document link. Both people have separate links in their hands, but those links open the same document. If one person edits the document, the other person sees the change because there was only one document.

Before storage terms enter the story, anchor two ideas. An object instance is the particular shared document itself. Two documents can contain the same words and still be two different documents. That difference is object identity. When this chapter later mentions heap storage, read it as the runtime-managed place where object instances normally live, not as the rule that explains behavior.

Boxing is like gift-wrapping one photocopy so it can sit on the shelf with other wrapped objects. The wrapped copy is separate from the original sheet. If you later write on the original, the wrapped copy does not update itself.

Here is the mapping for this chapter. A value-type variable holds the photocopy itself. A reference-type variable holds the link. The object instance is the shared online document. Boxing wraps a copied value-type photocopy into an object-shaped package. Strings are unusual shared documents: you can share their link, but you are not allowed to edit the document. Any "change" creates a new document.

Semantics first. Storage second.

Mental Model

C# types divide into value types and reference types. Structs, enums, numbers, bool, and char are value types. Classes, arrays, strings, interfaces, delegates, and ordinary records are reference types. An interface variable holds a reference to an object that provides that interface. A delegate is a reference-type object that represents a method call. A plain record is a record class unless you explicitly choose the value-type form, record struct.

A value-type variable contains its value for the purpose of assignment and passing. When you assign it to another variable, the language promise is copy semantics. The new variable receives an independent value. If the value type has fields, the fields are copied too.

That field copy is shallow. If a struct contains a number and a link to a mutable label object, copying the struct copies the number and copies the link. It does not copy the label object behind the link. After the copy, the two structs have separate value storage, but their label fields can still point at the same shared document.

Copying a value is not the same as copying everything reachable from that value.

For small values, copy semantics feels natural. For large structs, copying becomes a real cost, which is why structs are not automatically faster.

Treat this as a rule.

A reference-type variable contains a reference for the purpose of assignment and passing. The reference is the link, not the document. When you assign one reference variable to another, C# copies the link. It does not copy the object. After that assignment, two variables can refer to one object. Mutating the object through either variable changes the shared object.

Arrays fit this model cleanly. An array variable is a reference. Assigning the array variable copies the link to the same array object. The elements inside the array follow their own rules. If the array contains numbers, each element is a value. If the array contains objects, each element is a reference. The array itself is still a reference type.

Strings are reference types, but they are immutable. Immutable means the text inside a string object does not change after creation. When an operation appears to change text, it creates a new string object and points a variable at that new object. This is why repeated string concatenation creates new strings rather than extending one existing string in place.

A short storage primer helps keep the next part honest. The stack is method-call storage that is naturally tied to the current call and its local work. The heap is runtime-managed storage for objects that can outlive a single method call or be reached from many places. The garbage collector is the runtime memory cleanup system that later reclaims heap objects no longer reachable by the program.

Storage matters. It does not explain the promise.

Boxing happens when a value type must be treated as an object, or when it must be used through an interface view that requires an object-shaped value. Imagine a logging API that accepts general object values, and you hand it an integer. The integer is a value type, so the runtime makes a copy and wraps that copy in a separate object instance. The wrapper now has its own identity. Unboxing later copies the value back out.

The wrapper is not a live view of the original value. It is a wrapped photocopy.

The compiler and runtime preserve these meanings even when storage changes. A struct inside a class object lives as part of that object. A boxed struct lives inside a heap object. Under .NET 10, escape analysis can even allow some reference-type objects that never leave a method to avoid normal heap allocation. None of that changes the contract. Copy semantics and reference semantics are the model you reason from.

Walkthrough

Start with a Point value. Its X value is 1. This Point is a struct, so in our analogy it is a photocopy. You assign it to a second variable. The second variable receives its own photocopy of the Point, including the X value of 1.

Now you change the second Point's X value to 99. You wrote on the second photocopy. The first photocopy did not change. The first Point still has X equal to 1, and the second Point has X equal to 99.

That outcome is not a runtime accident. It is the language promise for value types. Roslyn compiles your assignment in a way that preserves the copy meaning, and the Common Language Runtime executes the resulting instructions without inventing sharing between those two variables.

Now repeat the story with a class-based point. Create one point object whose X value is 1. A first variable holds a link to it. You assign that variable to a second variable. The second variable receives a copy of the link, not a copy of the object.

There is still one shared online document.

You change the second class-based point's X value to 99. That means you followed the second link and edited the shared document. When you look through the first variable, you see the same document. The first variable now also observes X equal to 99.

The variable was copied. The object was not.

Method calls use the same rule, so keep the main picture in view. Passing a value type into a method gives the method its own photocopy unless you deliberately use a by-reference mechanism. Passing a reference type into a method gives the method its own copy of the link. The method can follow that copied link and mutate the shared object, but it cannot make your original variable point somewhere else.

By-reference passing is different because it gives the method access to the caller's variable slot. The method is no longer working only with its own photocopy or its own copied link. It can affect the caller's variable itself. That is a separate promise, and when you see it, read it as access to the original slot, not as ordinary assignment behavior.

Now return to the original Point struct whose X value is 1. You box it. The runtime gift-wraps a copy of that Point so it can sit on the object shelf. The boxed object contains X equal to 1. It is not the original Point. It is a separate runtime object with its own identity. It is a wrapped photocopy.

After boxing, you change the original Point's X value to 50. The original now reads 50, but the boxed copy stays stale at 1. Nothing about the gift wrap connects it back to the original sheet. When you later inspect the boxed value, you see the value that was copied at the moment of boxing.

This is why boxing matters even when it is invisible in source syntax. The source may read like one value is being treated more generally. The runtime reality is a new object containing a copied value. That object has allocation cost, identity as an object, and a value that no longer tracks the original. The garbage collector will eventually clean up that wrapper when the program can no longer reach it, but the allocation still happened.

Text adds one more twist. A string variable is a reference variable, so assigning it copies a link. Two variables can point at the same string object. But strings are immutable, so there is no operation that edits the existing text in place.

Imagine one string variable points at the text "blue." You assign it to another variable. Now both variables hold links to the same string object. Then you produce text that reads "blue sky" and store it in the second variable. You did not edit the original text. You created a new string object and moved the second variable's link to that new object. The first variable still points at "blue."

This is the correct way to understand string concatenation. Each new combined piece of text is a new string. In a small expression, that cost is usually harmless. In a repeated loop that keeps extending text, the pattern creates a trail of discarded string objects. The garbage collector will eventually clean them up, but the allocations were still real.

Arrays behave differently from strings even though both are reference types. Suppose two variables refer to the same array of numbers, and the third element holds 5. You change that element to 12 through the first variable. The second variable now also reads 12, because both variables share one array object. Arrays are mutable shared documents. Strings are immutable shared documents whose apparent changes create new documents.

There are also window types, Span of T and ReadOnlySpan of T, that let you look at a slice of existing memory without copying it. The full model for those arrives in the final chapter.

One final caution completes the model. Do not infer copy behavior from how large or small something feels. A variable of a large struct still follows value semantics. A variable of a tiny class still follows reference semantics. The shape of the type decides the contract. The runtime's storage choices are implementation details unless you are analyzing performance at a deeper level.

Story or Scenario

I once watched a small scheduling team chase a bug in a calendar import feature where several appointments changed labels after one cleanup step. Each imported appointment carried a start time, an end time, and a label metadata object with display text, source information, and a few flags. During cleanup, the code adjusted one label object so users could see that the appointment came from an external system. A developer expected only the cleaned-up appointment to change.

The bug report said otherwise. Several appointments showed the same adjusted label state.

The team first blamed the import file. Then someone noticed that those appointments shared one mutable label metadata object. Each appointment variable held its own link, but the links opened the same shared online document. The cleanup step edited the shared document through one appointment, so every appointment that held the same link saw the change.

The fix was not to "be careful with classes" in some vague way. The fix was to decide which label state should be shared and which label state should be independent. The team made label object creation explicit at the boundary where imported rows became appointments. After that, each appointment that needed independent label state got its own label object, and the shared metadata stayed intentionally shared.

Accidental sharing is a design bug, not a mystery.

Common Misconceptions

- "Value types live on the stack, and reference types live on the heap." This belief is tempting because it sounds concrete, but it is the wrong starting point. Value types promise copy semantics, and reference types promise shared-object semantics. A struct inside a class lives with that class object, a boxed struct lives in a heap object, and .NET 10 can optimize some short-lived reference objects without changing their meaning. Reason from semantics first.
- "Assigning a class variable copies the object." This is wrong because assignment copies the reference, not the object. Both variables can

point to the same object after assignment. Avoid the mistake by asking whether you copied a photocopy or copied a shared document link.

- "Copying a struct copies everything it can reach." This is wrong because struct copying is a shallow field copy. If one field is a reference to a mutable object, the copied struct gets a copied link to that same object. Keep the photocopy rule for the struct itself, and still inspect any shared links inside it.
- "Passing an object to a method gives the method total control over my variable." This confuses the link with the document. The method receives its own copy of the reference, so it can mutate the shared object but cannot replace your original variable's reference unless you explicitly pass the variable by reference. Separate "changing the object" from "changing which object a variable points to."
- "Strings act like value types because changing one string variable does not change another." The observed behavior is real, but the explanation is wrong. Strings are reference types. They feel copy-like in many cases because they are immutable, so apparent changes create new string objects. Remember that sharing still exists, but mutation does not.
- "Boxing keeps a live connection to the original value." This is wrong because boxing wraps a copy. The boxed value is a gift-wrapped photocopy placed on the object shelf. After boxing, changes to the original value do not update the boxed copy.
- "Arrays of numbers are value types because numbers are value types." This mixes the container with its elements. The array itself is a reference type. Assigning the array variable copies the link to the same array, even when each element inside the array is a value.

Summary

Value semantics and reference semantics tell you whether C# gives someone a photocopy or a shared online document link. Structs, enums, numbers, bool, and char copy their values. Classes, arrays, strings, interfaces, delegates, and ordinary records copy references to objects. Boxing gift-wraps a copied value so it can be treated as an object, and strings add the special rule that shared text cannot be edited in place. Keep asking one question as you read and write C#:

did this operation create an independent copy, or did it share access to the same underlying object?

Key Terms

- Value semantics: Assignment or passing gives the new variable its own value. Think photocopy.
- Reference semantics: Assignment or passing copies a link to an object. Two variables can point to the same shared online document.
- Value type: A type that follows value semantics for its variable. Structs, enums, numbers, bool, and char are value types.
- Reference type: A type that follows reference semantics for its variable. Classes, arrays, strings, interfaces, delegates, and ordinary records are reference types.
- Object identity: The runtime's idea that one allocated object is a distinct thing. Two references can point to that same identity.
- Heap storage: Runtime-managed memory where objects commonly live when they need identity, sharing, or a lifetime beyond one active method call. The garbage collector cleans this memory later.
- Stack storage: Short-lived storage tied to an active method call. Don't equate stack storage with value types; reason from semantics first.
- Shallow field copy: The normal copy of a struct copies its fields directly. If one field is a reference to a mutable object, the copied struct gets the same link, not a copy of everything that object can reach.
- Copy semantics: A copied value can change without changing the original value. This does not guarantee that every object reachable from the value was also copied.
- Shared-object semantics: Multiple references can reach one object. Mutating that object through one reference is visible through the others.
- By-reference passing: A method can receive access to the caller's variable slot instead of receiving a separate value or copied reference. Treat this as lending the original slot, not handing over a photocopy.

- Boxing: Wrapping a copied value type inside a separate runtime object so it can sit where general object references are expected. The boxed value is a gift-wrapped photocopy, not a live view.
- Unboxing: Taking the value back out of its boxed object wrapper. The value is copied out.
- Immutable: A property of an object whose contents do not change after creation. Strings are immutable, so apparent text changes create new string objects.
- Span of T: A stack-only window over contiguous memory. A span over the middle three entries in a five-item array views those entries without owning or copying them.
- ReadOnlySpan of T: A stack-only window over contiguous memory that does not allow modification through the window.
- Garbage collector: The runtime memory cleanup system for managed objects. It handles memory, not deterministic release of files, sockets, or other non-memory resources.
- Escape analysis: A runtime optimization that proves an object does not outlive its method. In .NET 10, that proof can let the runtime avoid normal heap allocation for some short-lived objects.

Mini Quiz

1. **You assign one struct variable to another, then change a field on the second variable. What should you expect?**

   A. Both variables show the changed value because structs share storage

   B. The first variable stays unchanged because the second variable received a copy

   C. The first variable changes only if the struct is small

   D. The result depends on whether the program is warmed up

2. **You assign one class variable to another, then mutate the object through the second variable. What happened?**

   A. The object was copied, then the copy was changed

   B. The reference was copied, and both variables can now reach the same object

   C. The runtime boxed the object before changing it

   D. The compiler converted the object into a value type

3. **A value type is boxed, then the original value is changed. What does the boxed object contain?**

   A. The updated original value

   B. A live link back to the original value

   C. The copied value from the moment boxing occurred

   D. No value until unboxing happens

4. **A struct contains a link to a mutable label object. You copy the struct, then edit the label object through the copy. What should you expect?**

   A. The original struct can observe the edited label because the link was copied

   B. The original struct cannot observe the edited label because all reachable objects were copied

   C. The label text changes only inside the copied struct because strings are mutable

   D. The runtime boxes the label before changing it

5. **Two variables refer to the same array of numbers. You change one element through the first variable. What does the second variable observe?**

   A. The changed element, because the array itself is a shared object

   B. The old element, because numbers are value types

   C. A boxed copy of the changed element

   D. A new array created by the assignment

6. **Which statement is the safest rule for reasoning about value types and reference types?**

   A. Value types always live on the stack, and reference types always live on the heap

   B. Small types copy, and large types share

   C. Reason from copy semantics and reference semantics before thinking about storage

   D. Runtime optimization changes the language meaning of assignment

Answers are provided in the Answer Key at the end of the book.

Reflection Prompts

- Describe a bug you've seen where two variables unexpectedly shared the same object.
- Identify a type in your current work that should behave like a photocopy rather than a shared document link.
- Compare how you think about arrays and strings after this chapter.
- Recall a time when performance advice about structs or classes focused too much on storage and not enough on semantics.

Chapter 4: Garbage Collection, Object Lifetimes, and Cleanup

What You Will Learn

- Understand the generational garbage collector as a lifetime system, not a mysterious background janitor
- Recognize why short-lived objects are usually cheap and long-lived accidental references are more costly
- Explain Generation 0, Generation 1, Generation 2, promotion, and the Large Object Heap
- Reason about why reachable objects cannot be collected, even when you are finished thinking about them
- Distinguish memory cleanup from deterministic release of files, sockets, database connections, and similar resources
- Treat finalizers as a fallback mechanism and reject GC.Collect as routine maintenance

Prerequisites

- Familiarity with the Chapter 1 habit of separating language promise, compiler behavior, and runtime behavior
- The Chapter 2 model of the Common Language Runtime as the execution engine that manages running code
- The Chapter 3 distinction between value semantics and reference semantics
- The Chapter 3 understanding that reference-type objects have identity and are allocated as runtime objects
- The Chapter 3 warning that storage location is not the same as semantic behavior

Why This Matters

Most C# developers learn early that .NET has a garbage collector, then stop at the comforting version of the idea: you create objects, and the runtime cleans them up. That is true, but it is not enough. The missing word is lifetime.

A program that allocates many short-lived objects can be healthy. A program that accidentally keeps old objects reachable can become slow, memory-hungry, and hard to diagnose. The difference is not morality. It is reachability over time.

This chapter arrives after values and references because garbage collection is mostly about reference-type objects and object identity. Chapter 3 taught you that a variable can hold a shared link to one object. This chapter teaches what happens when those links disappear, linger, or point at something too large to treat casually.

Lifetime is the real cost signal.

Core Analogy

The managed heap is the runtime-managed memory area used for managed object instances that require heap allocation. That includes ordinary reference-type instances, arrays, strings, and boxed values from Chapter 3. The garbage collector watches this managed heap and reclaims memory when objects are no longer reachable.

Think of the managed heap as an office.

New objects land on the desk. The desk is Generation 0, often called Gen 0. It holds the newest paperwork, and it gets swept constantly because most new papers are needed only briefly.

Objects that survive a desk sweep move to the drawer. The drawer is Generation 1, often called Gen 1. It holds things that were not temporary enough to throw away right away, but have not yet proved they belong in long-term storage.

Objects that keep surviving reach the archive room. The archive room is Generation 2, often called Gen 2. It holds long-lived objects, and checking it takes more effort, so the runtime does it less often.

Very large objects go to a special oversized storage area. That area is the Large Object Heap, often called the LOH. In .NET, objects whose runtime object size is 85,000 bytes or more belong conceptually in this oversized area. They are still managed objects, but their size changes the cost and timing of cleanup.

The garbage collector is the office service that sweeps the desk, checks the drawer, and occasionally visits the archive room and oversized storage. It does not clean up every kind of resource. It reclaims managed memory when objects are no longer reachable.

Files, sockets, database connections, and similar resources are different. They are more like borrowed office keys. You return them deliberately. You do not wait for the next desk sweep and hope someone notices.

Mental Model

The garbage collector is part of the Common Language Runtime. Its job is to reclaim managed memory from objects your program can no longer reach. It does not ask whether you emotionally consider an object done. It asks whether any live path still leads to that object.

Reachability is the central test. If a running method, a static field, a live object, a queued callback, or runtime bookkeeping for active work can still reach an object, the object stays. If no live path reaches it, the object is eligible for collection. Eligible does not mean collected immediately. It means the runtime is allowed to reclaim its memory during a collection.

Eligibility is permission, not a schedule.

Generations make this efficient. The runtime assumes that many new objects die young. This assumption is usually correct. Request buffers, temporary strings, short-lived lists, formatting helpers, and intermediate results often appear, serve one purpose, and vanish quickly.

So the garbage collector checks the desk often. A Generation 0 collection is usually cheap because the desk is small compared with the whole office, and because most paperwork on it is already trash by the time the sweep arrives. The runtime can clear a lot of new clutter without searching the archive room every time.

If an object on the desk is still reachable when the sweep happens, it survives. Survival changes its lifetime category. The object is promoted from Generation 0 to Generation 1.

Promotion is not a decision you make.

Promotion is the runtime noticing that an object has already survived one cleanup opportunity. Older generations are not checked during every Generation 0 sweep. They are checked during broader collections, and those broader collections cost more because the runtime examines more of the office. If an object keeps surviving those broader checks, it can be promoted again into Generation 2.

That expectation creates the practical rule. Short-lived allocation is often acceptable. Accidental long lifetime is where trouble begins.

Treat reachability as evidence, not intent.

An object becomes accidentally long-lived when some reference keeps it alive after its useful work is done. A cache that never evicts, an event subscription that is never removed, a static collection that grows forever, or a background service holding old request data can all keep objects reachable. With events, the publisher usually keeps a reference path to the subscriber through the subscription. If the publisher lives longer than the subscriber should, that path can keep the subscriber alive.

The garbage collector cannot reclaim reachable objects. It is not allowed to guess that you meant to let them go.

The Large Object Heap deserves separate attention. Objects of 85,000 bytes or more are large enough that moving and managing them has different costs. Large arrays and large strings are common examples. These objects still follow reachability rules, but large allocations create a different kind of pressure because each one consumes a noticeable amount of space. Large Object Heap collection is tied to Generation 2 collection behavior, so large objects are not treated like ordinary desk clutter.

Size changes cleanup economics.

Modern runtime optimization adds one useful wrinkle. In .NET 10, escape analysis can sometimes prove that an object never leaves a method, including some delegates and enumerators. When the runtime can make that proof, it can avoid putting that object on the managed heap at all. In the office analogy, some papers never reach the shared desk because the worker can finish with them locally.

This optimization is automatic. Write clear, idiomatic code and let the runtime take the win.

Memory is one side of cleanup. Non-memory resources are the other.

Unmanaged resources are resources outside the managed heap, often owned by the operating system or another external system. File handles, network sockets, database connections, operating system handles, and graphics resources fit this category. The garbage collector manages memory. It does not make those external systems unlimited.

IDisposable exists for deterministic release. Deterministic means you decide when the resource is released, not when the garbage collector eventually notices an object is unreachable. The disposal pattern, including calling Dispose when work is finished, gives your program a deliberate return point for borrowed resources.

Finalizers sit at the far end of the cleanup story. A finalizer lets an object perform last-chance cleanup before its memory is reclaimed, but it runs later, on runtime-controlled timing, and adds extra collection complexity. Treat finalizers as a safety net for types that own unmanaged resources directly. They are not a normal application cleanup pattern.

GC.Collect exists because the runtime exposes a manual collection trigger. In ordinary application code, it is almost never the right call. It interrupts the runtime's own judgment, can force expensive work at a bad time, and usually hides the real issue: object lifetimes are wrong, allocations are excessive, or deterministic cleanup is missing.

Do not manage the garbage collector by hand.

The diagram below shows the two outcomes that matter during a sweep. Unreachable objects leave the office and their memory can be reclaimed. Reachable objects stay in the office and may be promoted, which makes their lifetime more expensive if that reachability was accidental.

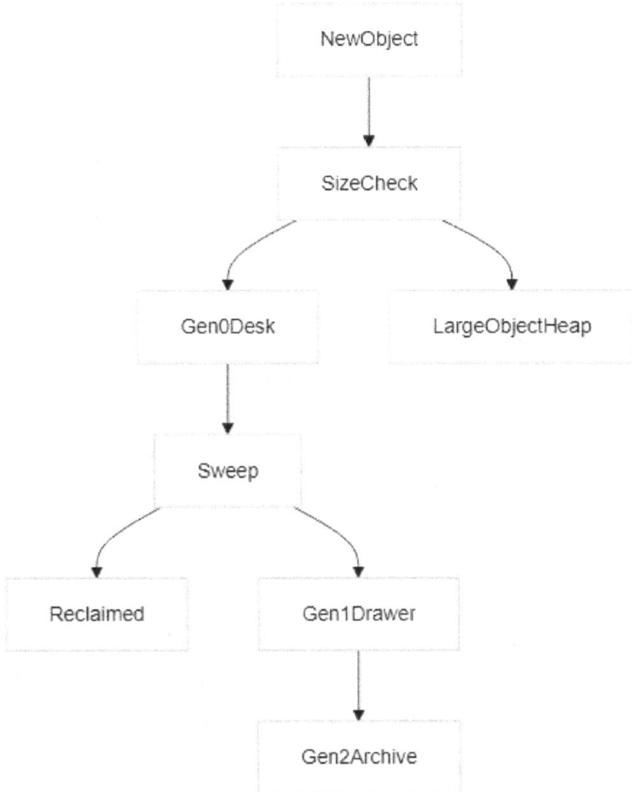

Walkthrough

You are handling one request in a service. During that request, the program creates several reference-type objects: a small list of parsed values, a few temporary strings, a short-lived helper object, and a response model. In the office analogy, these new objects land on the desk. They are Generation 0 objects.

While the method is running, those objects are reachable. Local variables can reach them. Other objects created during the request can reach them. The response model may refer to the list, and the list may refer to several items. The garbage collector sees live paths through the office paperwork, so nothing on the desk gets thrown away yet.

The method finishes. Most of the temporary objects are no longer reachable. The local variables that pointed to them are gone. No static field stores them. No live object refers to them. The next time the runtime performs a desk sweep, those unreachable Generation 0 objects can be cleared cheaply.

That is the happy path.

Now change one detail. The response model is placed into a shared in-memory cache because another part of the program wants to reuse it briefly. A healthy cache has an eviction rule, such as a size limit, an expiration policy, or a clear owner that removes entries. This cache has no such rule.

Give every cache an exit policy.

The request method ends, but the cache still has a reference to that model. The model is still reachable. Anything it references is also reachable. During the next Generation 0 collection, the garbage collector cannot reclaim it.

The object survives the desk sweep. The runtime promotes it from Generation 0 to Generation 1. In the office, the paper moved from the desk into the drawer because it proved it was not immediate trash.

More requests arrive. More desk sweeps happen. The cached model remains reachable because the cache still holds it. During broader collections, the runtime also checks older generations. If the model survives those checks, it can be promoted from Generation 1 to Generation 2. In the office, the paper has reached the archive room.

This does not mean the object is bad. Some objects should live a long time. Application configuration, shared lookup data, single long-lived services, and reusable metadata often belong in the archive room. The problem is not age by itself. The problem is accidental age.

A month-end reporting service taught me this distinction sharply: its largest retained objects were not leaks in the garbage collector, they were closed report models still reachable from an unbounded recent-documents cache.

Now add a large allocation. One request creates a byte array large enough to cross the 85,000-byte threshold. Conceptually, that object does not sit on the ordinary desk with small paperwork. It goes to oversized storage, the Large Object Heap.

If the large object becomes unreachable quickly, the runtime can eventually reclaim it. If it remains reachable through a cache, a static field, or a long-lived object, it occupies oversized storage for as long as that path exists. The cost feels different because the object is large. A few such objects can matter more than thousands of tiny temporary objects.

Size changes the stakes.

Next, the request opens a file to read uploaded content. The object representing that file access may be managed, but the file handle behind it belongs to the operating system. The garbage collector can reclaim managed memory when the object becomes unreachable. That is not the same as promptly returning the file handle.

The correct plan is deterministic cleanup through IDisposable. You release the resource when the work is done, including when the work fails or an error path interrupts the normal flow. In office terms, you return the borrowed key before leaving the room. You do not drop the key somewhere on the desk and trust that a future sweep will return it at a convenient time.

Imagine skipping that release. The file object eventually becomes unreachable. Most objects do not have finalizers, so unreachable managed memory is often the whole cleanup story. If this particular type does have a finalizer, it may eventually run and clean up the handle. Every word in that chain matters. Eventually is not a scheduling guarantee. During the delay, the process may hold more files, sockets, or connections than it should.

This is why finalizers are a fallback, not the plan. They are useful when a type directly owns unmanaged resources and needs last-chance protection. They are not a substitute for deterministic cleanup by the caller.

Finally, suppose someone notices memory rising and adds a call to GC.Collect after every request. That is like ordering a full office inspection after each conversation because some papers once piled up. The runtime already knows how to sweep the desk frequently. Forcing a collection can promote objects at awkward times, burn processor time, and hide the actual lifetime mistake.

The better investigation starts with reachability. Which objects are living longer than intended. Which cache lacks an eviction rule. Which event subscription keeps an object reachable. Which large object is retained after the request ends. Which resource needs deterministic cleanup, even when failure paths run.

Find the lifetime problem. Do not shake the whole office.

Story or Scenario

A small team maintained a desktop reporting tool used by accountants at month end. The app opened several large reports at once, then let users export them to files. During testing, memory climbed steadily, and exported files sometimes stayed locked until the application closed.

One developer suggested forcing garbage collection after every export. The first test looked encouraging because memory dipped after the forced collection. Then the application felt uneven. Some exports paused at awkward moments, and file locks still appeared under heavier use.

The team traced object lifetimes instead. The report previews were stored in a recent-documents list with no limit, so large report data stayed reachable long after users closed the preview. The export path also failed to release a file resource deterministically when an error occurred. The garbage collector was not confused. The office was keeping papers in the archive room and leaving borrowed keys on the desk.

They fixed the recent-documents lifetime and made file release deterministic. Memory stopped climbing during normal use, and file locks disappeared without routine GC.Collect calls. The lesson was direct: the garbage collector reclaims unreachable memory, but it does not correct your ownership decisions.

Common Misconceptions

- Garbage collection means memory is freed as soon as an object is no longer used. This belief is tempting because C# removes the need for manual memory release. The correct understanding is that unreachable objects become eligible for collection, and the runtime chooses when to collect them. Avoid this mistake by thinking in terms of reachability and collection timing, not immediate cleanup.
- Value types live on the stack, so garbage collection only matters for classes. This is wrong because storage location is not the same as semantic behavior, as Chapter 3 established. A value can be inside a heap object, and reference-type objects can sometimes be optimized by the runtime. Avoid the shortcut. Reason first about semantics, then about lifetime and reachability.

- Long-lived objects are always a problem. This is tempting because Generation 2 collections cost more than Generation 0 collections. The corrected view is that intended long-lived objects are normal, while accidental long-lived objects create pressure. Treat configuration and stable shared data differently from stale request data, forgotten event subscribers, and unbounded caches.
- The Large Object Heap is just a bigger Generation 0. This is wrong because very large objects are managed with different costs and are collected along with older-generation collection work. The 85,000-byte threshold matters because large allocations consume meaningful space quickly. Avoid casual large allocations in hot paths, and avoid retaining large buffers longer than needed.
- IDisposable is about helping the garbage collector free memory faster. This confuses two cleanup systems. IDisposable is for deterministic release of non-memory resources such as files, sockets, database connections, and handles. Avoid the confusion by asking whether the object owns something outside managed memory. If it does, release it deliberately.
- Finalizers are a normal cleanup strategy. This belief is common because finalizers appear to promise automatic last-minute cleanup. The correct understanding is that finalizers run on runtime-controlled timing, delay reclamation, and add collection complexity. Use them as a safety net in resource-owning types, not as the everyday cleanup path in application code.
- GC.Collect fixes memory problems. This is the wrong instinct. It is tempting because it can make memory graphs move during a test, but it does not remove reachable objects or close resources you failed to release deterministically. Treat GC.Collect as almost never appropriate in routine application code. Look for lifetime problems instead.

Summary

Garbage collection in .NET is a lifetime system for managed heap memory. New managed objects land on the desk in Generation 0, survivors move to the drawer in Generation 1, long-lived objects reach the archive room in Generation 2, and very large runtime objects go to the Large Object Heap. The garbage collector reclaims memory only when objects are unreachable, so accidental references matter more than good intentions. Use short-lived objects freely when they fit the design, give caches and subscriptions clear lifetimes, release non-memory resources deterministically through IDisposable, and do not treat GC.Collect as routine maintenance.

Key Terms

- Garbage collector: The part of the Common Language Runtime that reclaims managed memory from objects your program can no longer reach.
- Managed heap: The runtime-managed area where managed object instances that require heap allocation are allocated and tracked for garbage collection. This includes reference-type instances and boxed copies of value types.
- Reachability: The rule the garbage collector uses to decide whether an object must stay alive. If any live path can still reach an object, the object remains.
- Generation 0: The newest generation of managed objects. It is collected often because many new objects become unreachable quickly.
- Generation 1: The middle generation for objects that survived at least one earlier collection. It acts as a transition area between short-lived and long-lived objects.
- Generation 2: The oldest generation for long-lived managed objects. It is collected less often because checking it costs more.
- Promotion: The runtime's movement of a reachable object from a younger generation to an older generation after it survives collection.
- Large Object Heap: The managed heap area used for objects whose runtime size is 85,000 bytes or more. These objects are still collected by reachability rules, and their collection is tied to Generation 2 collection behavior.
- Deterministic release: Cleanup that happens at a chosen point in program flow rather than at a later time chosen by the garbage collector.

- Unmanaged resource: A resource outside managed memory, such as a file handle, socket, database connection, or operating system handle. The garbage collector manages memory, not the timely release of these resources.
- IDisposable: The .NET pattern for releasing non-memory resources such as files, sockets, database connections, and operating system handles. Treat disposal as calling for cleanup when the work is finished, including failure paths.
- Finalizer: A last-chance cleanup mechanism that runs on runtime-controlled timing before an object's memory is reclaimed. It is a safety net, not a normal cleanup plan, and it delays reclamation while adding collection complexity.
- Event subscription: A connection where a publisher keeps a reference to a subscriber's handler. That connection can keep the subscriber alive until the subscription is removed or the publisher becomes unreachable.
- GC.Collect: A manual request for garbage collection. It exists, but routine application code should almost never use it.

Mini Quiz

1. **What does the garbage collector use as its main test for whether an object must remain alive?**

   A. Whether the object was created recently

   B. Whether the object uses a large amount of memory

   C. Whether any live path can still reach the object

   D. Whether the developer considers the object finished

2. **A request creates several short-lived helper objects. The method finishes, and no live object points to those helpers. What should you expect?**

   A. They become eligible for collection

   B. They immediately move to Generation 2

   C. They must be released through IDisposable

   D. They remain alive until the process exits

3. **Why can an unbounded cache cause memory pressure?**

   A. It forces every object into the Large Object Heap

   B. It keeps references to objects that would otherwise become unreachable

   C. It prevents value types from being copied

   D. It disables tiered just-in-time compilation

4. **What is the best mental model for IDisposable?**

   A. It tells the garbage collector to collect faster

   B. It releases non-memory resources at a chosen time

   C. It moves objects from Generation 2 back to Generation 0

   D. It prevents objects from ever being allocated

5. **A large byte array crosses the 85,000-byte runtime size threshold and remains reachable through a static field. What is the key issue?**

   A. The object cannot be managed by the runtime

   B. The object is copied every time the static field is read

   C. The object remains alive because a live path still reaches it

D. The object is automatically cleaned up at the next Generation 0 collection

6. **A long-lived publisher has an event subscription to a short-lived subscriber. The subscriber is no longer used anywhere else. What can happen?**

   A. The subscriber can remain alive because the publisher still has a reference path to it

   B. The subscriber is immediately moved out of managed memory

   C. The subscription forces the subscriber onto the Large Object Heap

   D. The garbage collector ignores event subscriptions during reachability checks

Answers are provided in the Answer Key at the end of the book.

Reflection Prompts

- Describe a cache, list, or event subscription you have seen that could accidentally keep objects alive.
- Identify a place in one of your applications where deterministic release matters on both success and failure paths.
- Compare a healthy long-lived object with an accidental long-lived object from a system you know.
- Recall a time when memory increased during a run. Describe whether reachability, large objects, or missing resource cleanup was the more likely cause.

Chapter 5: Types, Records, Equality, and Operators

What You Will Learn

- Understand a type as a semantic contract, not just a container for data
- Distinguish object identity from equality based on meaningful contents
- Recognize why ordinary classes and records compare differently by default
- Explain how structs and record structs connect equality to value semantics
- Understand the contract between Equals and GetHashCode
- Treat operators as declared behavior that belongs to a type's public meaning
- Recognize C# 14 partial constructors and user-defined compound assignment operators as tools for organizing and customizing type behavior without weakening the contract

Prerequisites

- Familiarity with the three-layer reasoning habit from Chapter 1: language promise, compiler behavior, and runtime behavior
- Familiarity with value semantics and reference semantics from Chapter 3
- Familiarity with object identity and shallow field copy from Chapter 3
- Awareness of boxing and unboxing from Chapter 3 as background for value types
- The idea from Chapter 4 that runtime allocation and lifetime are separate from semantic meaning
- Familiarity with partial types: one type whose definition is written across more than one source part but combined into one type by Roslyn

Why This Matters

Equality bugs are rarely loud at first. They sit quietly in comparisons, tests, lookups, change tracking, and business rules until a program treats two things as the same when the domain says they are different, or treats two equivalent things as different when the domain says they match.

C# gives you several ways to define types: classes, structs, interfaces, enums, records, and record structs. They do not all mean the same thing. A class often says, "this object has identity." A record often says, "these contents are the meaning." A struct says, "copy this value." An interface says, "anything that can perform this role is acceptable." Those choices affect how your program behaves long before performance enters the discussion.

Operators belong in the same design conversation. If a type says two money amounts cannot be combined across currencies, an addition operator must not quietly ignore that rule. If construction has validation rules, partial constructors must still preserve one construction meaning. If a compound assignment updates a value, that update must honor the same type contract as every other operation.

Treat equality as design, not decoration.

This chapter belongs here because Chapters 3 and 4 separated meaning from storage. Now you need the next layer: how a type declares what its instances are, how they behave, and what it means for two of them to count as equal.

Core Analogy

A type is a courthouse filing rulebook.

The rulebook defines what kind of document something is. It says whether a filing gets its own official case number, whether matching written contents are enough to treat two filings as equal, and which official actions the clerks are allowed to perform on that filing.

In this analogy, the type is the rulebook. Runtime object identity is the courthouse case number. Equality is the comparison rule. GetHashCode is the shelf label clerks use to group filings quickly. Operators are official clerk actions.

A class is usually a filing where the official case number matters by default. Two separate filings are not the same just because their pages contain matching words. A record is a filing form where the comparison rule usually focuses on the written fields. Two separate record filings can still have different runtime identities, because they are different objects, but equality can ignore that identity and compare contents instead.

A struct is a filing copied by value, like the photocopy model from Chapter 3. A record struct is still copied by value, but its rulebook also says that matching contents determine equality.

Equal filings must receive matching shelf labels. Operators must behave like authorized clerk actions, not back doors around the rulebook.

The rulebook matters more than the paper.

Mental Model

A type is a promise about meaning. It tells readers, Roslyn, and the Common Language Runtime what kind of thing an instance represents and which operations are valid for that thing.

Classes define reference types. As you saw in Chapter 3, a class variable holds a link to an object, not the object itself. By default, ordinary class equality follows identity. Two variables are equal when they refer to the same runtime object. Two different objects with matching fields are still different objects unless the type customizes equality.

Equals is the equality rule. For ordinary classes, Equals uses identity by default unless the type author overrides or otherwise customizes that behavior. That default is not a failure. It is the correct rule for many things with ongoing identity, such as accounts, windows, connections, and editable documents.

Records change the default expectation. A plain record is a record class, so it is still a reference type and still has runtime object identity. Its generated equality, however, is value-based. In courthouse terms, the record still has a case number, but the comparison rule usually reads the form fields instead.

Relevant contents means the contents that participate in the equality rule. For generated record equality, that means the equality members Roslyn includes when it creates the record's comparison behavior, commonly the data that defines the record's declared shape. Custom equality can change the rule, but custom behavior then becomes part of the public contract. The compiler follows the record definition, not later business intent that exists only in someone's head.

Write the rule down in the type.

Mutable records require discipline. If equality-relevant contents change after a record is placed into a hash-based collection, its shelf label can change while the filing is already on the shelf. Lookup failures then feel mysterious, because the filing is still present but no longer lives under the label the collection expects. Values used for equality should usually be stable.

Records pair that stability with a with expression, the copy-with-changes tool. A with expression takes an existing record and produces a new record that differs only in the members you name, while the original is untouched. It is filing an amended form: the clerk copies the original filing, changes only the named fields, and stamps a new filing. If an order record has applicant Rivera and fee amount 50, copying it with a fee amount of 75 yields a second record with Rivera and 75, the original still reads Rivera and 50, and the two compare unequal because an equality member now differs. This nondestructive mutation is how you change a record value without disturbing the version other code already holds.

Structs define value types. Assignment and passing copy the value, as Chapter 3 described with photocopies. A struct has no separate object identity in the ordinary class sense. Its meaning travels with the copied value. By default, the runtime compares ordinary structs by value, member by member, so two structs with matching fields already count as equal under Equals, unlike classes. Customizing Equals and GetHashCode on a struct is about making that comparison faster and intentional while honoring the contract, not about turning identity into value equality. Ordinary structs still do not automatically receive the full record-style equality surface. In particular, equality operators are not assumed for every ordinary struct. A record struct combines copy behavior with generated value-based equality, including equality-style operators that should agree with Equals.

Storage is not the contract.

Enums define named intended values. They work well when the domain has a fixed set of named labels, such as filing status. Do not overstate the guarantee. An enum is backed by an underlying numeric value, and it can hold an unnamed value unless the program validates it. The rulebook names the intended choices; validation enforces whether only those choices are accepted.

Interfaces define roles. An interface does not say what an object is made of. It says what behavior a type must provide to be treated as capable of a role. In the courthouse, an interface is like a desk rule that says, "any filing that can be reviewed through these official actions qualifies for this process."

Roslyn carries these choices into the assembly as type information, members, and callable behavior. The runtime then executes the resulting calls and comparisons. The three-layer habit from Chapter 1 still applies: the language promise says what equality and operators mean, Roslyn emits the machinery that represents that meaning, and the runtime performs the work.

Equality has two major questions. First, are these the same filing by identity? Second, do these filings count as equal under the rulebook? Object identity answers the first question. Equals answers the second. Sometimes those answers match. Often, they should not.

GetHashCode adds a practical rule. If Equals says two instances are equal, GetHashCode must produce the same hash code for both. The reverse is not required. Two unequal filings can share a shelf label, just as two courthouse folders can be placed in the same cabinet section and still need a clerk to inspect the pages.

Operators also belong to the rulebook. They are not magic punctuation. They are declared behavior. When a type defines an operator, it tells the language what a familiar action means for that type. A money type can define addition in a way that preserves currency rules. A measurement type can define comparison in a way that respects units. Equality-style operators should agree with Equals, or the type teaches two conflicting comparison rules.

Do not let syntax outrank meaning.

An invariant is a rule that must remain true for a valid instance of a type. A filing fee cannot be negative. A date range cannot end before it starts. A currency amount cannot forget its currency. Constructors, methods, equality, and operators must preserve those invariants, or the type's rulebook stops being trustworthy.

C# 14 adds two features that fit this chapter's theme. Partial constructors let construction behavior be split across parts of a partial type while preserving one construction meaning. User-defined compound assignment operators let a type define a compound update action directly, rather than relying only on a separate operation followed by assignment. Both features are organizational and expressive tools. They don't excuse a vague contract.

Walkthrough

Start with one courthouse process: importing permit filings into a review system.

The courthouse receives two permit filings from separate envelopes. Filing A is created as one runtime object. Filing B is created as another runtime object. Both pages say applicant name Rivera, filing kind permit, business case number 1001, and fee amount 50.

The pages match. The runtime identities do not.

Under an ordinary class rulebook, Filing A and Filing B are separate filings by default. Even if every visible field matches, including the business case number printed on the page, ordinary class equality says they are not equal unless the type author customized equality. The official courthouse case number in the analogy is runtime object identity, not a field that happens to be printed on the form.

This default is useful when identity matters. A live claim, an editable permit, or an open review ticket often has a continuing life beyond its current field values. Two editable filings with matching text are not automatically the same filing. The rulebook says, "different runtime identity, different filing."

Now the courthouse introduces a standardized import form. For this import step, the rulebook says that applicant name, filing kind, business case number, and fee amount define equality. Filing C and Filing D arrive separately with matching contents. They are still separate runtime objects if the import form is a record class, but the equality rule treats them as equal because the contents that matter match.

That distinction is the whole point.

The team chooses the record-shaped rulebook for the import model because the import step cares about duplicate content, not object identity. Later, when a filing becomes an editable review case, the team uses an identity-heavy class because the case now has a life of its own. One courthouse process can contain both ideas, but each type needs one coherent rulebook.

Bring the shelf label into the same scenario. The import system groups filings before checking exact equality. GetHashCode supplies that shelf label. If Filing C and Filing D are equal under Equals, they must receive the same shelf label. If they do not, the courthouse can put equal filings in different shelf areas and fail to find a duplicate that is present.

Unequal filings can share a shelf label. That is allowed. It only means the clerk must inspect more than one filing in that shelf group. Equal filings with different shelf labels break the courthouse.

Next, the courthouse handles the filing fee. A fee amount type defines which clerk actions are allowed. Clerks can combine two compatible fees, compare two fees, or apply an approved adjustment. These actions are operators in the type's public rulebook.

The operator cannot contradict the rest of the type. If the ordinary method rules reject combining fees in different currencies, the addition operator must reject that too. If Equals says two fee values are equal, equality-style operators should say the same thing. A developer should not need to guess which door into the courthouse gives the real answer.

C# 14 user-defined compound assignment operators make the update-style action explicit. Instead of treating a compound update as only a separate operation followed by assignment, the fee type can declare what that update means directly. The clerk action becomes part of the rulebook.

That does not make the action automatically safe. It makes the action visible. The operator still must preserve the type's invariants, such as a nonnegative fee and a valid currency.

Now add construction. The permit filing type is partial, which means one type has its rulebook written in more than one place and Roslyn combines those parts into one type. A generated part may describe the shape of the filing, while a hand-written part supplies validation or construction behavior.

C# 14 partial constructors fit that arrangement. A constructor's declaration and implementation can be split across parts of the partial type. The rules are exact: a partial constructor has exactly one defining declaration and exactly one implementing declaration, and only the implementing declaration may chain to another constructor through a this or base initializer. The filing still enters the courthouse through one construction rule. The paperwork may be organized across two desks, one declaring and one implementing, but the completed filing must obey one rulebook.

Partial constructors are about splitting the work, not splitting the truth.

On one permit import service, I found duplicate detection failing because the import model used an identity-heavy class while the business process expected matching form contents to collapse together.

Here is the practical instinct: when you create or review a type, decide what kind of courthouse filing it represents. If identity matters, an ordinary class with identity-based equality may be the right default. If contents define meaning, a record or record struct often says that more directly. If the type supports operators, those operators must behave like official clerk actions, not shortcuts around the rules.

The type's contract is the source of truth.

Story or Scenario

A claims team built a small review tool for insurance filings. Each imported claim note had a claim number, an author, a timestamp, and the note text. The first version used ordinary classes everywhere. During a cleanup task, the tool tried to remove duplicate notes by comparing note objects. Nothing disappeared. The notes looked identical on screen, but the program treated each one as a separate filing with its own runtime identity.

The team first blamed the cleanup task. Then one developer traced the meaning of the type. The note was not supposed to be an identity-heavy live object during import. For that specific step, a note was a filing form whose author, timestamp, and text defined equality. I watched a similar review stall for half an afternoon because the team kept staring at matching field values instead of asking which rulebook the type had chosen.

The team introduced a record-shaped import model and kept the identity-heavy class for the editable claim note stored later. That split changed the design conversation. The import model compared contents. The stored claim note kept identity. Later, when fee totals were added, the team defined the allowed clerk actions on the money type instead of scattering arithmetic rules around the tool.

The fix was not "use records everywhere." The fix was choosing the right filing rulebook for each concept.

Common Misconceptions

- "Classes compare their fields by default." This belief is tempting because the debugger shows matching field values side by side. Ordinary class equality is identity-based unless customized, so treat matching fields as unrelated to equality until the type's rulebook says otherwise.
- "Records are just shorter class syntax." This is wrong because records change the expected equality model. A plain record is still a reference type with identity, but its generated equality is value-based, so use records when contents are the meaning, not just to reduce typing.
- "Record equality follows whatever the business later decides is relevant." This fails because generated equality follows the members Roslyn includes in the record's equality behavior. If business meaning changes, change the type contract deliberately.
- "Enums can only contain their named values." This is wrong because an enum can hold an unnamed underlying value unless the program validates it. Treat enum names as intended choices, not as automatic runtime validation.
- "Value types are equal because they live on the stack." This repeats the storage-first mistake from Chapter 3. Value types follow value semantics, and storage location does not define equality. Reason from copying and the type's equality rule, not from stack and heap folklore.

- “Equal objects can return different hash codes as long as Equals is correct.” This breaks the contract. Equal objects must produce equal GetHashCode results, or hash-based lookup behavior becomes unreliable. Design Equals and GetHashCode as a matched pair.
- “Operators are harmless convenience.” This is a dangerous habit. Operators are public behavior attached to the type’s meaning. If an operator violates the same rules as the type’s methods and equality, the type becomes misleading.
- “Partial constructors create separate construction meanings.” They do not. C# 14 partial constructors split declaration and implementation across a partial type, but callers still see one construction contract. Use them to organize construction, not to hide conflicting initialization rules.
- “User-defined compound assignment operators are just syntax polish.” This misses the design point. In C# 14, a type can define a compound update action directly, which makes the intended behavior explicit. The action still must preserve the type’s invariants.

Summary

A type is a courthouse filing rulebook. It defines what kind of filing an instance is, whether identity or contents drive equality, which comparison rule Equals follows, which shelf label GetHashCode supplies, and which official actions operators are allowed to perform.

Classes, structs, interfaces, enums, records, and record structs give you different ways to express meaning. Ordinary classes start with identity-based equality. Records and record structs make value-based equality central. Structs keep the copy behavior from Chapter 3. Interfaces describe roles, and enums name intended values that still need validation when unnamed underlying values matter.

The main habit is to decide equality as part of the type’s design, not after the fact. If two instances count as equal, their hash codes must match. If operators exist, they must honor the same rulebook. C# 14 partial constructors and user-defined compound assignment operators give you more ways to organize and express type behavior, but they do not change the obligation: one type, one coherent contract.

Key Terms

- Type: A named rulebook that defines what an instance means and which operations are valid for it.
- Class: A reference type whose ordinary equality starts with object identity. Use a class when a concept has a continuing runtime identity beyond its current field values.
- Struct: A value type that follows copy semantics. An ordinary struct has value semantics, but it does not automatically get the same generated equality operators as a record struct.
- Record: A record class whose generated equality usually compares relevant contents instead of object identity. Relevant contents are the members the compiler includes in generated equality, unless the type customizes that behavior.
- Record struct: A value type that combines copy semantics with record-style equality based on relevant contents. It is useful for small value-shaped concepts where contents define equality.
- Enum: A value type that names intended values from a fixed set of labels. An enum can still hold unnamed underlying values unless validation prevents them.
- Interface: A type contract that describes a role a type can perform. It says what behavior must be available, not how the implementing type stores its data.
- Object identity: The runtime's recognition that one allocated object is a distinct thing. In the courthouse analogy, identity is the case number assigned to that specific file.
- Equals: The equality rule for a type. Ordinary classes use object identity by default unless equality is customized.
- GetHashCode: The method that supplies a hash value used by hash-based collections as a shelf label for lookup. A matching hash code doesn't prove equality, but equal instances must produce the same hash code.
- Operator: Declared behavior that gives a familiar operation meaning for a specific type. Operators are official clerk actions in the type's rulebook, not decoration.

- Equality operator: An operator that expresses equality or inequality for a type. It should agree with Equals so the type does not present two conflicting comparison rules.
- Invariant: A rule that must remain true for a type to stay valid. Constructors, methods, equality, and operators should all preserve the same invariants.
- Partial type: One type whose rulebook is written in more than one declaration part. The parts combine into one type contract.
- Partial constructor: A C# 14 feature that lets construction behavior be split across parts of a partial type while still presenting one construction contract.
- User-defined compound assignment operator: A C# 14 feature that lets a type define an update-style operator action directly. It must preserve the same meaning and invariants as the rest of the type.

Mini Quiz

1. **Two ordinary class instances contain the same field values, but they were created separately. What does default equality usually say about them?**

   A. They are equal because their fields match

   B. They are not equal because they are different objects

   C. They are equal if their hash codes happen to match

   D. They are not valid until GetHashCode is customized

2. **A team models a search filter where the selected fields define the entire meaning of the value. Which type choice best expresses that equality by default?**

   A. An ordinary class with identity-based equality

   B. An enum

   C. An interface

   D. A record or record struct

3. **Why must Equals and GetHashCode be designed together?**

   A. GetHashCode decides whether two instances are equal

   B. Equals runs only after GetHashCode returns different values

   C. Equal instances must produce matching hash codes for hash-based lookup to work correctly

   D. Unequal instances are forbidden from sharing the same hash code

4. **A status is represented by an enum with three named labels, but a value arrives from stored numeric data. What should you remember?**

   A. The enum can still hold an unnamed underlying value unless validation prevents it

   B. The enum can hold only the three named labels

   C. The enum becomes a record when the value is unnamed

   D. GetHashCode rejects unnamed enum values automatically

5. **What does a C# 14 partial constructor allow?**

   A. A type to have multiple conflicting construction meanings

   B. Construction behavior to be split across parts of one partial type

C. A record to become a struct at runtime

D. GetHashCode to be generated separately from Equals

6. **A money type refuses to combine different currencies in its normal methods but allows an operator to combine them silently. What is the design problem?**

   A. The operator is too slow

   B. The operator changes the object's storage location

   C. The type should have been an enum

   D. The type has two conflicting rulebooks

Answers are provided in the Answer Key at the end of the book.

Reflection Prompts

- Describe a type you've used where identity mattered more than matching field values.
- Identify a type in your work that would be clearer if contents defined equality.
- Compare a class and a record you have seen, and explain what each one's filing rulebook seemed to say.
- Recall a bug involving comparison, lookup, duplicate detection, or enum validation, and connect it to the type's rulebook.

Part III: Abstractions in Motion

Chapter 6: Generics as Real Runtime Types

What You Will Learn

- Understand reified generics, the idea that a filled generic rulebook remains real to the runtime
- Distinguish a generic rulebook template from a working rulebook with its type category filled in
- Explain why a generic list of integers stores integer elements without boxing each one
- Recognize constraints as eligibility promises about what type arguments must support
- Understand generic interfaces as reusable role contracts that stay precise about type
- Reason about covariance and contravariance as controlled substitutions for declared generic roles
- Explain why C# 14 can name an unbound generic type template without filling its type slot

Prerequisites

- Familiarity with the three-layer reasoning habit from Chapter 1: language promise, compiler behavior, and runtime behavior
- Familiarity with the Common Language Runtime from Chapter 2 as the execution engine that works with real runtime type information
- Familiarity with value semantics, reference semantics, and boxing from Chapter 3
- Familiarity with the Chapter 5 model of types as courthouse filing rulebooks, and interfaces as roles rather than storage

Why This Matters

Generics sit under much of the C# you already write. Collections, interfaces, query pipelines, asynchronous results, and many library application programming interfaces, or APIs, depend on the same idea: write one shape of behavior, then let that behavior become precise for a specific type. Without the right model, generics look like fancy placeholders. That model is too weak.

The stronger model is that .NET generics are reified. A generic type with its slots filled is a real runtime type. That fact explains why a generic list of integers can remain type-safe without gift-wrapping every integer in a boxed object, and why the runtime can still know what kind of thing it is handling.

Chapter 5 gave you types as courthouse filing rulebooks. Generics extend that courthouse model. Instead of writing a separate rulebook for every case category, the court writes a rulebook template with blank slots. Once the slot is filled by a type category, the result is not a suggestion. It is a working rulebook.

Core Analogy

Generics are courthouse rulebook templates with blank slots.

The generic type definition is the blank rulebook template. It says, "This filing process works for a case category to be named later." A type argument fills the blank slot with a type category, such as integer entries, text entries, customer entries, or invoice entries. It does not fill the slot with one particular value. The constructed generic type is the real working rulebook the court receives after the blank is filled.

Constraints are eligibility rules. They say which case categories are allowed into a particular template. Generic interfaces are recognized court roles, such as a role that provides entries or a role that accepts entries. Variance is a controlled substitution stamp. It allows one filled role to stand in for another only when the role declares that substitution and the promise of the role remains safe.

This analogy builds directly on Chapter 5. A type is still a courthouse filing rulebook. A generic type is a rulebook template that becomes a specific rulebook when the court fills in its blanks with type categories.

Do not think text substitution.

Mental Model

A generic type definition is the courthouse's blank rulebook template. It declares one or more type slots and describes behavior in terms of those slots. The blank is a type category to be supplied later, not a value waiting to be inserted.

An unbound generic type is the template named without filling its slots. This is the template as a recognizable court form. C# 14's nameof on unbound generic types works with that idea: the language can name the template itself without pretending the court has already chosen integer entries, customer entries, or any other category.

An open generic type is a generic rulebook that still has at least one unfilled type slot. It is not yet a normal working rulebook for everyday filing. The clerk can talk about the template, but the clerk cannot use a blank slot as if it were a finished case category.

When all required slots are filled with concrete type arguments, you get a closed constructed generic type. A generic list whose slot is filled with the integer type becomes one real working rulebook. The same generic list whose slot is filled with the text type becomes another. They share the template, but they are not the same filing category.

Use "closed" when precision matters.

The language promise is type safety. If the rulebook says it stores integer entries, the compiler prevents you from placing text entries into that cabinet. Roslyn carries that meaning into Intermediate Language. The Common Language Runtime then executes with enough type information to preserve the promise.

Reification means the runtime has real knowledge of constructed generic types. The runtime is not looking at a vague untyped container and hoping the compiler already checked everything. It understands the filled rulebook. That is why a generic list of integers can store integer elements as integers instead of treating each value as a generic object.

This matters for boxing. Chapter 3 taught that boxing gift-wraps a copied value type so it can sit on the shelf with objects. A non-generic object-based container has to treat everything as object-shaped, so an integer value needs wrapping. A generic list whose slot is filled with the integer type has an integer-specific filing rulebook. It does not need to gift-wrap each integer element just to store it.

On a telemetry importer that still used object-based event buckets, I traced a burst of boxing back to small numeric identifiers that lost their category too early.

Runtime implementation still has engineering freedom. Reification is the promise that constructed generic types are real to the runtime, not a promise that every filled rulebook always receives a completely separate pile of native machine code. The runtime can share native machine code where sharing preserves behavior, especially across reference types. It can use more specialized handling for value types when their exact representation matters.

The promise is semantic, not mechanical.

Constraints narrow what can fill the blank. A template can say, "Only case categories that perform a certain interface role may enter," or "Only case categories with a public parameterless constructor may enter." Value types satisfy that public parameterless constructor constraint. Once an eligibility rule exists, the compiler can allow behavior that depends on the promise. Without the constraint, the blank slot holds too many possible categories, so the compiler must reject assumptions.

That authority matters.

Generic interfaces turn templates into roles. A concrete filing cabinet can provide customer entries without exposing how it stores them. Another component can accept customer entries without caring where they came from. The generic interface lets the role stay precise about the entry category while hiding the cabinet design.

Constraints and interfaces solve different problems. A constraint controls who is eligible to enter a template. A generic interface describes a role that a finished type can play.

Variance controls substitution between related constructed interface or delegate types. It does not say all related types are interchangeable. It requires three things: the interface or delegate must declare the variance, the type categories must have a compatible reference-type conversion, and the direction of use must remain safe. Generic classes, including generic lists, are invariant unless you view them through a variant interface they implement.

Treat variance as permission, not inheritance.

Start with the category relationship. A premium customer entry belongs to the broader category of customer entry. Every premium customer entry is a customer entry, but not every customer entry is premium. Variance rules only apply to compatible reference-type relationships like that, not to value-type conversions such as integer to a larger numeric type.

A producer role gives values out. If a declared covariant role only produces premium customer entries, it is safe to use it where a producer of customer entries is expected, because every premium customer entry is still a customer entry. That is covariance. The substitution moves from more specific to more general for a producing role.

A consumer role takes values in. If a declared contravariant role can accept customer entries, it is safe to use it where a consumer of premium customer entries is expected, because premium customer entries are within the broader category it already accepts. That is contravariance. The substitution moves from more general to more specific for a consuming role.

C# declares covariance with the out keyword on a generic interface's type parameter, matching the producer direction where values flow out. It declares contravariance with the in keyword, matching the consumer direction where values flow in.

A role that both produces and consumes the same type slot usually cannot vary safely. If the same court window both hands out and accepts entries of one category, substituting a different category risks breaking one side of the promise. In that case, the role stays invariant. No substitution stamp is granted.

C# 14 adds a small but telling convenience: nameof on unbound generic types. The language can refer to the name of the rulebook template itself, the form with blank slots, without demanding a closed constructed type first. That feature does not change how generics work. It reflects the same mental model: the template has a recognizable identity, even before the court fills every blank.

Walkthrough

Imagine the courthouse needs one filing process for many case categories. The court handles integer entries, text entries, customer entries, and audit entries. Writing a separate filing rulebook for every category would create repetition, and repetition invites disagreement. One clerk changes the integer rulebook, another forgets to change the text rulebook, and soon the court has two filing processes that should have stayed aligned.

The courthouse creates one rulebook template. It has a blank slot for the case category. The template says how to store items, how to retrieve them, and how to preserve the category promise. The blank does not mean “anything goes.” It means “this rulebook becomes exact when the slot is filled by a type category.”

First, the court fills the slot with the integer type. Now it has a closed constructed rulebook for integer entries. This is not a vague shared pile of objects. It is a real filing category at runtime. The compiler knows that the cabinet accepts integer entries, and the runtime understands that this is the integer version of the generic template.

Now the court fills the same template with the text type. A second closed constructed rulebook appears, this time for text entries. The two rulebooks come from the same template, but they govern different case categories. The integer cabinet does not accept text entries. The text cabinet does not produce integer entries.

Precision is the point.

Next, you place three integer entries, the small integers 7, 12, and 30, into the integer cabinet. Because the cabinet’s rulebook is built for integer entries, the integers enter as values of their own kind. They do not need to be gift-wrapped as boxed objects. Chapter 3’s boxing model still applies, but the generic rulebook avoids the situation that causes boxing. The court does not say, “Put every entry into a generic object envelope.” It says, “This cabinet is for integer entries.”

That is the practical payoff of reified generics. The type promise stays specific, and value types avoid the extra wrapper that an object-based design would require. You keep type safety and avoid unnecessary boxing at the same time.

Now the court adds a special filing process. This process does not work for every category. It needs each case category to provide a certain capability, such as the ability to identify itself. The template gains an eligibility rule. Only categories that satisfy that rule may fill the blank.

The constraint changes what the clerks may assume. Without the eligibility rule, a blank case category is too unknown. The filing process cannot safely ask for identifying behavior because some possible category lacks it. With the rule in place, the compiler can trust the promise and allow the process to use that role. The constraint is not decoration. It gives the rulebook legal authority to make a stronger assumption.

Name the capability in the constraint.

After constraints, the court separates storage from roles. One filing cabinet stores customer entries in one internal arrangement. Another stores the same kind of entries differently. A clerk does not need to know either design. The clerk only needs a recognized court role: something that can provide customer entries.

That role is a generic interface. It says, "I provide entries of this category," without saying what the cabinet looks like inside. The interface is generic because the role stays category-aware. A provider of customer entries and a provider of audit entries perform the same kind of role, but they do not provide the same kind of entry.

Then substitution enters the story. Suppose premium customer entries belong to the broader category of customer entries. A clerk asks for a provider of customer entries. You hand the clerk a provider of premium customer entries. This is safe only because the provider role has declared covariance, and because premium customer entries have a compatible reference-type relationship to customer entries. The role only produces entries, so the controlled substitution stamp can be applied.

Now reverse the direction. A clerk needs a consumer that can accept premium customer entries. You offer a consumer that accepts customer entries. This is safe only because the consumer role has declared contravariance. A consumer that accepts the broader category can accept the narrower category. The role only consumes entries, so the substitution stamp works in the other direction.

The court refuses to stamp unsafe substitutions. A generic class such as a list does not become variant just because its type categories are related. If a role both provides and accepts entries of the same category, substitution can break the rulebook. A cabinet that accepts customer entries is not safe to treat as a cabinet that provides only premium customer entries. It may hand back a customer entry that is not premium. A cabinet that provides premium customer entries is not safe to treat as one that accepts all customer entries. It may reject some customer entries. Producing and consuming pull in opposite directions, so no variance stamp is granted.

Keep roles narrow when substitution matters.

Finally, the court needs to print the name of a template in an official notice. It does not need the integer version or the text version. It needs the name of the template form itself. C# 14 supports that idea with nameof on unbound generic types. The language can name the open template without pretending a specific case category has already filled the slot. Using nameof on the unbound generic list type evaluates to the bare name, the word List, with no type arguments attached.

The whole walkthrough has one thread: generics preserve precision across reuse. The court gets one template, many real filled rulebooks, eligibility rules when needed, role contracts across different cabinets, and controlled substitution only when the promise remains safe.

Story or Scenario

A billing team builds a shared audit trail for several services. One service tracks invoice events. Another tracks payment events. A third tracks refund events. The first version uses a loose object-based container because it feels flexible. Within two weeks, the team finds casts scattered through the code, a few runtime failures in test, and extra boxing around small numeric event identifiers.

During a design review, one developer redraws the system as a courthouse template. The audit trail is not “a box of objects.” It is a rulebook template with a blank slot for the event category. The invoice service gets a real audit trail for invoice events. The payment service gets a real audit trail for payment events. The refund service gets its own filled rulebook too.

I once watched a review like this change the vocabulary of a team in one meeting. The useful phrase was not “make it generic.” The useful phrase was, “What category fills the slot?”

Then the team adds an eligibility rule. Only event categories that expose an audit identity can use the shared filing process. The compiler now protects the assumption that every stored event can be identified. Later, reporting code depends on a producer role rather than a concrete audit cabinet, so different storage designs can feed the same report.

The insight changes the design language. The team stops saying “generic means flexible” and starts saying “generic means reusable without losing precision.”

Common Misconceptions

- Generic types are just compile-time text replacement. This belief is tempting because the source code shows a blank-looking slot. It is wrong because .NET generics are reified, and constructed generic types exist as real runtime rulebooks. Avoid the mistake by asking which filled rulebook the runtime is dealing with.
- A generic list of integers stores boxed integers internally. This belief comes from older object-based container habits. The correct understanding is that a generic list filled with the integer type stores integer elements without boxing each one. Watch for boxing when a value type is treated as object or as an interface in a context that requires wrapping, not merely because generics are involved.
- An open generic type and a closed constructed generic type are basically the same thing. This is wrong because the open type still has at least one blank slot, while the closed constructed type has all required slots filled with concrete type arguments. Treat the open form as the courthouse template that still needs completion and the closed form as the working rulebook.
- Constraints are only documentation. This belief is common because constraints read like descriptions of what the caller should provide. They are stronger than that. Constraints let the compiler enforce eligibility and allow the generic body to rely on promised capabilities.

Use constraints when the template needs a real capability, not when you only want to explain intent.

- Variance means related generic types can freely substitute for one another. This is wrong because variance requires a declared variant interface or delegate, a compatible reference-type conversion, and a safe direction. Generic classes such as generic lists are invariant. Keep producer and consumer roles separate in your head.
- Interfaces erase the concrete type so safety is lost. This confuses hiding implementation with losing type information. A generic interface can hide the cabinet design while preserving the entry category. Use the interface role to reduce coupling, not to throw away precision.

Summary

Generics let C# reuse a rulebook without weakening its promises. The generic type definition is the courthouse template with blank slots. An open generic type still has at least one blank. A closed constructed generic type is the real working rulebook created when all required slots are filled with concrete type arguments. Because .NET generics are reified, the runtime still understands the filled rulebook, which is why a generic list of integers can store integer elements without boxing each one.

Constraints act as eligibility rules, generic interfaces express reusable court roles, and variance is a controlled substitution stamp granted only when the role declares it and the substitution remains safe. C# 14 nameof on unbound generic types fits the same model: the language can recognize the template form itself, even before any specific case category fills the blank.

Key Terms

- Reification: Reification means .NET generics exist as real constructed types at runtime. The runtime knows the filled generic rulebook instead of treating generic information as erased placeholder text.
- Generic type definition: A generic type definition is the reusable rulebook template with one or more open slots. It describes the type before any type category fills those slots.

- Open generic type: An open generic type still has at least one unfilled slot. It is recognizable as a template or partly filled rulebook, but it is not the same as a closed constructed generic type.
- Unbound generic type: An unbound generic type names the generic template itself without supplying type arguments. C# 14 nameof on unbound generic types uses this idea.
- Type argument: A type argument is the specific type category used to fill a generic slot. The slot is filled by a type, not by an individual value.
- Constructed generic type: A constructed generic type is formed when type arguments are supplied to a generic type definition. When all required slots are filled with concrete type arguments, it is a closed constructed generic type.
- Closed constructed generic type: A closed constructed generic type has no unfilled generic slots. A generic list of integers and a generic list of text are different closed constructed generic types.
- Constraint: A constraint is an eligibility rule for a generic slot. It tells the compiler which capabilities a type argument must provide before it can be accepted.
- Constructor constraint: A constructor constraint requires the type argument to have a public parameterless constructor. Value types satisfy this requirement.
- Generic interface: A generic interface is a reusable role contract that remains precise about the type it works with. It hides implementation details without throwing away the type category.
- Variance: Variance is the rule system that allows certain generic interface and delegate substitutions when they remain type-safe. It requires declared variance on the interface or delegate and a compatible reference-type conversion.
- Covariance: Covariance allows a producer of a more specific reference type to stand in where a producer of a more general reference type is expected. It is safe because every produced specific item is also a general item.
- Contravariance: Contravariance allows a consumer of a more general reference type to stand in where a consumer of a more specific

reference type is expected. It is safe because the broader consumer can already accept the narrower input.

- Invariance: Invariance means no substitution is allowed between related constructed generic types. Generic classes such as generic lists are invariant, and roles that both produce and consume the same type slot are usually invariant too.
- Nameof on unbound generic types: Nameof on unbound generic types is a C# 14 feature that lets the language name the generic template rulebook without filling its type slots first.

Mini Quiz

1. **What does it mean that .NET generics are reified?**

   A. Generic type information exists only while Roslyn compiles the source

   B. Constructed generic types exist as real type rulebooks at runtime

   C. Generic types always become object-based containers internally

   D. Generic type slots are replaced by source text before compilation

2. **A team uses a generic list of integers. What should they expect about boxing for the integer elements stored inside that list?**

   A. Every integer element is boxed because all generics store objects

   B. The integer elements are stored in that specific generic list without boxing

   C. Boxing happens only after the garbage collector promotes the list

   D. The runtime boxes integer elements during warm-up and removes boxing later

3. **In the courthouse analogy, what is a constraint?**

   A. A shelf label used for hash-based lookup

   B. A controlled substitution stamp for producer and consumer roles

   C. An eligibility rule that limits which case categories can fill a blank slot

   D. A copied filing form that no longer tracks the original

4. **A reporting component only needs something that provides customer case files, and it should not care how those case files are stored. Which concept best matches that design?**

   A. Generic interface

   B. Boxing

   C. Large Object Heap

   D. Partial constructor

5. **A declared covariant provider of archived customer files is used where a provider of general customer files is expected. Why is this safe?**

A. Because consumers always allow broader substitution

B. Because constructed generic types are all interchangeable at runtime

C. Because generic interfaces erase the actual file category

D. Because the provider only gives values out, and every archived customer file is also a general customer file

6. **What does C# 14 nameof on unbound generic types allow?**

   A. Naming the generic template rulebook without filling its type slots

   B. Creating a closed constructed generic type without choosing type arguments

   C. Turning a generic interface into a class

   D. Avoiding constraints when a generic body needs promised capabilities

Answers are provided in the Answer Key at the end of the book.

Reflection Prompts

- Describe a place where you currently use a generic collection and name the closed constructed generic rulebook it represents.
- Identify an application programming interface (API) you've used where a constraint would make the required capability clearer.
- Compare a producer role and a consumer role from a system you know, and decide which declared variance direction would be safe for reference types.
- Recall a time you saw casts around object-based storage, and explain how a generic type could have preserved precision.

Chapter 7: Delegates, Closures, and Events

What You Will Learn

- Understand delegates as type-safe containers for callable behavior
- Distinguish a delegate type, a delegate value, and the callable target it points to
- Recognize when a method or lambda is being stored, passed, returned, or invoked later
- Predict when Roslyn creates a closure backpack for captured variable slots
- Explain why captured variables are shared slots, not frozen snapshots
- Understand events as controlled publish and subscribe behavior over delegates
- Connect event subscriptions to reachability and object lifetime
- Apply delegate variance only when the delegate type allows it
- Recognize how C# 14 refines lambda parameters and partial events without changing the model

Prerequisites

- The language promise, compiler behavior, and runtime behavior reasoning habit from Chapter 1
- Roslyn lowering source intent into Intermediate Language from Chapter 1
- Reference semantics and shared-object reasoning from Chapter 3
- The managed heap and reachability model from Chapter 4, especially for captured objects and event subscriptions
- Type contracts, interfaces, and invariants from Chapter 5
- Generics, generic interfaces, covariance, contravariance, and invariance from Chapter 6

Why This Matters

C# lets you hand behavior around. You can store a payment retry action for later, pass a sorting rule into a collection operation, subscribe a dashboard panel to a notification, or choose a validation rule at runtime. That feels normal after you have written C# for a while, but it hides one of the most useful shifts in the language: behavior can become a value.

When developers do not understand that shift, they misread lambdas, closures, and events. They expect a captured variable to freeze its current value. They forget that an event subscription can keep an object reachable. They expose delegate fields as if they were harmless callbacks, then discover outside code can replace the whole notification list.

Chapter 6 gave you generic roles and variance. Now those ideas start moving. A delegate is not just a type shape. It is a route for real behavior.

Treat behavior as data with a call button.

Core Analogy

This chapter uses one courier-system analogy.

A delegate type is an approved delivery route. It defines what kind of package the route accepts and what kind of reply, if any, comes back. The route is type-safe, so a caller cannot send the wrong kind of package and hope for the best.

A delegate value is a dispatch ticket for that route. It is the actual thing you store, pass, return, or invoke later. The ticket says which courier destination should be called through the approved route.

A callable target is the courier destination. It can be a named method. It can be a lambda hired on the spot. For an instance method, the destination includes both the method and the receiving object that owns that method.

A closure is the backpack the courier carries. When a lambda uses a variable from the surrounding method, Roslyn gives the courier a backpack that carries that variable slot. The backpack does not hold a photograph of the variable's old value. It holds access to the variable itself.

An event is a guarded subscription desk. Subscribers sign up at the desk by adding dispatch tickets. The publisher can call everyone on the list, but outside code does not get to grab the list directly, clear it, replace it, or raise the notification as if it owned the publisher's voice.

The analogy has one limit. Real couriers are people with independent judgment. Delegates and lambdas do exactly the callable work they represent. The point of the analogy is routing, dispatch tickets, backpacks, and controlled sign-up, not human decision-making.

Mental Model

A delegate is a type-safe callable reference. It is not a string name. It is not a loose memory address. It is a typed route that says callable behavior with this accepted input and expected result may travel here.

Keep three things separate in your head. The delegate type is the route. The delegate value is the dispatch ticket that travels through your program. The callable target is the destination the ticket points to. Once you make that separation, delegates stop feeling like syntax magic.

A callable target can be a named method. It can also be a lambda, which is inline callable behavior created at the point of use. Once a lambda fits a delegate route, the resulting delegate value can be stored in a variable, passed to another method, returned from a method, or invoked later. Common delegate families such as Func and Action are still part of this same model: typed routes for callable behavior.

Creating behavior is not invoking behavior.

Roslyn lowers this source-level idea into ordinary runtime pieces. When no outside variables are captured, a lambda can often become a method-like callable target with little extra baggage. When the lambda reads or changes a variable from the surrounding scope, the situation changes. Roslyn must preserve the language promise that the lambda uses that same variable, even if the surrounding method call has already ended.

That is where the backpack appears.

A closure is compiler-generated support for captured variables. The backpack contains captured variable slots. If a delegate still points to callable behavior that needs those slots, the closure support remains alive after the original method call returns. The method's normal local work has finished, but the captured slot has been moved into support that can outlive the call.

Captured variables are not snapshots.

Two lambdas that capture the same variable share access to the same slot. If the variable changes, every courier looking into that backpack sees the changed value. This is not a timing accident. It is the language promise.

Reference semantics from Chapter 3 and reachability from Chapter 4 matter here. The closure backpack is an object the runtime can keep alive. If a delegate still points to callable behavior that needs the backpack, the backpack remains reachable. If the backpack contains references to other objects, those objects remain reachable too.

Lifetime follows reachability.

Instance-method delegates have a second lifetime detail. A delegate value for an instance method carries the callable destination and the receiving object. If a delegate points to a dashboard panel's instance method, the delegate can keep that dashboard panel reachable. The route needs both the method and the object that receives the call.

Events build on delegates but add a controlled surface. A public delegate field is like leaving the dispatch list on the counter. Outside code can assign a new list, clear the old list, or replace the publisher's subscribers with a completely different set. That breaks the publisher's control over its own notification mechanism.

Do not expose the dispatch list.

An event puts the dispatch list behind a guarded subscription desk. Outside code can subscribe or unsubscribe. Raising an event means the publisher invokes the current subscriber list to announce that something happened. Outside code does not raise the event, and outside code does not replace the entire list.

Many events use multicast delegates. A multicast delegate is one delegate value with an internal invocation list pointing to several callable targets. When the publisher raises the event, each signed-up target is called in the order held by that delegate list. The publisher should not need to know who subscribed. Subscribers should not need to know who else is on the list.

That separation is the whole point.

Delegate variance completes the variance model from Chapter 6, but only when the generic delegate type declares variance and reference-type conversions make the substitution safe. A delegate that produces a result can follow covariance rules for its result. A courier that promises to bring back a more specific kind of result can safely stand in where a more general result is expected. A delegate that consumes an argument can follow contravariance rules for its parameter. A courier willing to accept a more general kind of package can safely stand in where a more specific package will be sent.

Producer direction and consumer direction still govern safety.

C# 14 refines the surface without changing this model. Parameter modifiers on simple lambda parameters let compact lambda parameter lists express details such as reference passing or output-style passing without switching to a more formal parameter spelling. In plain terms, the small lambda form can now say more clearly how a parameter travels into or out of the callable target.

Partial events are also a C# 14 feature. They let an event declaration and its implementation be split across parts of a partial type while still presenting one event contract. This helps when generated code and human-written code share responsibility for the same type. Neither feature changes what delegates, closures, or events are. They make the route signs and subscription desk easier to express.

Walkthrough

You are working on a payments system. A retry coordinator scans failed receipts, builds retry actions, and later runs those actions. When a retry finishes, the coordinator publishes a notification so the dashboard, audit log, and cache can respond.

Start with the retry action route. The delegate type is the approved route. It says what input the retry action accepts and what result, if any, the coordinator expects back. The receiving code knows that route. It does not need to know the original method name, only the accepted inputs and expected result promised by the delegate type.

Now choose the first callable target. A named method already exists on a payment service, and it performs one retry. You do not call it immediately. You create a delegate value that points to that method and hand the dispatch ticket to the retry coordinator.

At the language level, C# promises that this callable value can be invoked through the delegate route. At the compiler level, Roslyn records enough information for the dispatch ticket to point at the callable destination. At the runtime level, the Common Language Runtime invokes that destination when the delegate is called.

The behavior moved without being executed first.

Next, the coordinator adds a small logging rule with a lambda. The lambda is the courier hired on the spot. It fits the same callable system because the route defines the required shape. The coordinator can store that delegate value, pass it to another component, return it from a setup operation, or invoke it later when the retry actually runs.

Creating the lambda does not run the retry. It creates callable behavior that can run later.

Now add captured state. The retry coordinator scans three failed receipts and creates three logging lambdas during a loop. The loop counter begins at zero. During the first trip through the loop, you create a lambda that answers with the counter. During the second trip, you create another. During the third trip, you create another. Later, after the scan has finished, you ask each lambda for its answer.

Many developers expect zero, one, and two.

The actual answer is three, three, and three.

All three couriers reached into the same backpack, because couriers hired in the same scope share one backpack when they capture the same variable; each carries its own only when each captures its own copy. Inside that backpack was the same captured counter variable, not three separate photographs of earlier values. By the time you asked the couriers to answer, the loop had finished and the shared counter had reached three. Each courier looked into the backpack and reported what was there.

The result follows from the language promise. A closure carries the variable slot, not the value you happened to see when the lambda was created. Since the three lambdas captured the same changing slot, they all observed the final value in that slot.

Fix the scenario by giving each loop iteration its own local copy. On the first iteration, that local copy holds zero. On the second, a new local copy holds one. On the third, another new local copy holds two. Each lambda captures its own copy for that iteration.

Now the couriers carry separate backpack contents. When you ask them later, they answer zero, one, and two.

The fixed version works because you changed what was captured. You did not ask the closure to become a snapshot machine. You created separate variable slots, so each backpack had its own slot to carry. One reassurance: since C# 5, the iteration variable in a foreach loop is already a fresh variable on every pass, so this trap belongs to counter loops you advance yourself and to manually shared variables, not to foreach.

Now add the completion notification. The retry coordinator publishes an event when a receipt retry finishes. The event is the guarded subscription desk. The dashboard subscribes with an instance method. The audit log subscribes with a named method. The cache subscribes with a lambda that records a small refresh decision.

Each subscription adds a dispatch ticket to the event's internal list. If the dashboard uses an instance method, its delegate value carries both the method and the dashboard panel object that receives the call. The publisher does not just keep a method pointer. It keeps a callable destination, and that destination can include an object.

This matters before the first notification is ever raised. If the retry coordinator lives for the whole application session and the dashboard panel closes without unsubscribing, the coordinator's event list can still reach the dashboard panel through the delegate value. The garbage collector does not know that the panel is no longer useful. It only knows the publisher can still reach it.

Unsubscribe when lifetime demands it.

When a retry finishes, the coordinator raises the event. That means it invokes the current multicast delegate value behind the subscription desk. The dashboard updates its display, the audit log writes an entry, and the cache refreshes. The coordinator does not call those components by name. It follows the route and calls the signed-up dispatch tickets.

The event boundary protects the publisher's invariant from Chapter 5. Outside code can sign up. Outside code can leave. Outside code does not clear the whole list, replace the list, or raise the notification on the publisher's behalf. A public delegate field would allow those mistakes because outside code would have direct assignment access to the dispatch list.

Now carry variance through the same system. Suppose one notification route only produces a result for callers to read. If the generic delegate type declares the result position covariant, and the reference-type conversion is safe, a courier that returns a more specific receipt result can stand in where a more general payment result is expected. The caller still receives something it can treat as the general kind.

A route that only consumes input is flexible in the other direction, when the delegate type declares the parameter position contravariant and the reference-type conversion is safe. If the publisher will send a specific receipt notification, a subscriber willing to accept a more general payment notification is safe. The subscriber can handle the specific notification because it already accepts the broader category.

Trouble begins when you ignore direction. A route that both consumes and produces the same type usually cannot vary freely, because safety would have to work both ways at once. That is why Chapter 6 treated producer and consumer roles carefully. Delegates make those roles concrete.

Finally, apply the C# 14 refinements to the same payments system. A compact lambda can now express certain parameter modifiers directly in its simple parameter form, such as when the callable route needs reference-style parameter behavior. The courier route can say how the package is handed over without forcing a more verbose lambda shape.

Partial events help when the payment notification type is split across generated and human-written parts. One part can declare the event surface, and another can provide the implementation details, while users of the type still see one guarded subscription desk. The courier system stays the same. The route signs and desk construction become clearer.

Story or Scenario

A small payments team had a background job that retried failed receipts. The job scanned three failed receipt records, created retry actions, and ran those actions after the scan completed. Each retry action used the correct receipt object for the payment call, so the actual retries went to the right service with the right receipt data.

The log looked wrong. Every retry reported the same final scan number. Two developers first suspected the logger. Another suspected the scheduler. Neither was the source of the bug.

The bug was in the backpack.

The payment call used a per-action receipt value, but the diagnostic lambda had captured the loop's changing scan counter. The couriers were not carrying three independent counter values. They were all reaching into the same backpack and reading the same slot after the scan had moved on. The team fixed it by creating a separate local value for each iteration before hiring the logging lambda.

A week later, the same team found a second issue in a dashboard event. Old dashboard panels stayed alive after users closed them because they were still subscribed to a long-lived publisher. The guarded subscription desk had kept their couriers on the list.

Their takeaway was clear: closures carry variable slots, and event desks keep subscribers reachable.

Common Misconceptions

- A delegate is just the name of a method. This is tempting because delegates often point at named methods. The correct model is a type-safe callable container on an approved route. Avoid the mistake by separating the delegate type, the delegate value, and the callable target.

- Creating a lambda runs the lambda. This belief comes from reading a lambda as if it were an immediate instruction. Creating a lambda hires the courier and creates callable behavior. Invoking the delegate sends the courier. Keep creation and invocation separate.
- A lambda is less real than a named method. This is wrong because both can become callable targets for a delegate route. A lambda is inline behavior that fits a route; a named method is preexisting behavior that fits a route. Judge them by the delegate shape they satisfy.
- A captured variable is a snapshot of the value at the time the lambda is created. This is wrong because the closure backpack carries the variable slot itself. If the variable changes before the lambda runs, the lambda sees the changed value. Avoid relapse by saying “captured slot” instead of “captured value.”
- Three lambdas created in a loop automatically remember zero, one, and two. This expectation is common because each lambda is created during a different loop pass. If they capture the same loop counter slot, they all answer three after the loop finishes. Create a separate local copy per iteration when each lambda needs independent state.
- Events prevent lifetime problems. Events control who can subscribe and who can raise, but they do not erase references. A long-lived publisher with subscribed delegates can keep subscriber objects reachable. Treat subscriptions as lifetime relationships and remove them when the subscriber’s lifetime ends.
- A public delegate field is equivalent to an event. This is wrong because outside code can replace or clear a public delegate field. An event restricts outside code to subscribing and unsubscribing, while the publisher controls raising the notification.
- Delegate variance means any similar callable shape can substitute for another. This is wrong because variance applies only when the generic delegate type declares it and the reference-type conversion is safe. Results follow the covariant producer direction, and parameters follow the contravariant consumer direction. Keep the direction in view before trusting a substitution.
- C# 14 partial events change what an event is. They do not. Partial events refine how event surfaces and implementations can be split

across partial type parts. The event remains a guarded subscription desk built on delegate behavior.

Summary

Delegates let C# treat behavior as a value without abandoning type safety. In the courier system, the delegate type is the approved route, the delegate value is the dispatch ticket, the callable target is the courier destination, a closure is the backpack that carries captured variable slots, and an event is the guarded subscription desk that controls publish and subscribe behavior.

The core habit is to ask what is being carried and who can still reach it. If a lambda captures a changing variable, it sees the variable slot, not an old photograph. If a delegate points to an instance method, it can keep the receiving object reachable. If an event keeps a subscriber on its list, the subscriber remains reachable. Delegate variance follows declared producer and consumer directions, and C# 14's refinements make callable and event surfaces clearer without changing the underlying model.

Key Terms

- Delegate: A type-safe callable reference. It defines the approved route for calling behavior with a specific input shape and result shape.
- Delegate value: A particular callable package that can be stored, passed, returned, or invoked later. It points to a callable target, and for an instance method it also carries the receiving object.
- Callable target: The method or lambda body that a delegate value reaches when invoked. The receiving code knows the delegate route, not necessarily the target's internal details.
- Lambda: Callable behavior created at the point where it is needed. Creating a lambda prepares behavior; invoking the delegate that holds it runs that behavior.
- Closure: Compiler-generated support for a lambda that uses variables from an outer scope. In this chapter's analogy, it is the backpack the courier carries.

- Captured variable: A variable from an outer scope that a lambda uses. The closure carries the variable slot itself, not a frozen copy of the value, and that slot can remain alive after the original method call has ended.
- Event: A controlled publish and subscribe surface built on delegates. It lets outside code subscribe or unsubscribe without giving outside code permission to replace, clear, or directly invoke the publisher's notification list.
- Raising an event: The publisher's act of notifying current subscribers through the event's delegate list.
- Publisher: The object or component that owns an event and raises it when something meaningful happens.
- Subscriber: The object or component that signs up to be notified by an event.
- Multicast delegate: One delegate value with an internal invocation list that points to several callable targets. Events commonly use this so one publication can notify several subscribers.
- Delegate variance: The safe substitution rules for delegate types based on producer and consumer direction. Result types follow covariance, and parameter types follow contravariance, but only when the delegate type declares variance and the needed reference-type conversions are valid.
- Parameter modifiers on simple lambda parameters: A C# 14 feature that lets simple lambda parameters, meaning lambda parameters without explicit types, express parameter-passing details such as by-reference, output, or read-only input behavior directly.
- Partial event: A C# 14 feature that lets an event declaration and implementation be split across parts of a partial type while preserving one event contract.

Mini Quiz

1. **What is the best mental model for a delegate?**

   A. A text name that identifies a method

   B. A storage container for object fields

   C. A background thread that runs later

   D. A type-safe route to callable behavior

2. **A lambda reads a variable from the method that created it. What does the closure carry?**

   A. A snapshot of the variable's value at creation time

   B. The variable slot used by the lambda

   C. A copy of the whole method

   D. A separate thread reserved for the lambda

3. **Three lambdas are created in a loop and all capture the same loop counter. After the loop finishes at three, what do they report when called later?**

   A. Zero, one, and two

   B. One, two, and three

   C. Three, three, and three

   D. The result is unpredictable

4. **Why can an event subscription keep an object alive?**

   A. The publisher can still reach the subscriber through the delegate list

   B. The event automatically stores every subscriber in Generation 2

   C. Events disable the garbage collector for subscribed objects

   D. Lambdas always allocate objects on the Large Object Heap

5. **What is the difference between creating a lambda and invoking it?**

   A. Creating a lambda runs it immediately, while invoking it only stores it

   B. Creating a lambda prepares callable behavior, while invoking it runs the behavior

   C. Creating a lambda requires an event, while invoking it requires a class

D. Creating and invoking a lambda always happen at the same time

6. **Which statement best matches delegate variance?**

   A. Any delegate with a similar name can substitute for another

   B. Contravariance means result types become more specific

   C. Variance applies only to events, not delegates

   D. Variance is safe only when producer and consumer direction allow it

Answers are provided in the Answer Key at the end of the book.

Reflection Prompts

- Describe a time when you passed behavior into another operation, then name the delegate route it followed.
- Identify a lambda you have written that captured an outer variable, then describe what its backpack carried.
- Recall an event subscription in a real application and name the publisher, subscriber, and lifetime relationship.
- Compare creating a lambda with invoking it, using an example from work you have done.

Chapter 8: LINQ and Deferred Execution

What You Will Learn

- Understand Language Integrated Query, or LINQ, as a recipe that usually describes work before it performs work
- Recognize enumeration as the moment a deferred LINQ query actually runs, often through a loop or an operation that asks for results
- Explain why later changes to a source can appear in a query result
- Predict why repeated enumeration can repeat filtering, sorting, reshaping each item, and work sent to another system
- Distinguish in-memory LINQ from queryable LINQ that a provider, such as a database provider, translates
- Decide when materialization, forcing a query now into a concrete collection, is the right choice because you need a stable snapshot

Prerequisites

- Familiarity with generics as real runtime types from Chapter 6, especially generic sequences and type arguments
- Familiarity with delegates and lambdas from Chapter 7, because in-memory LINQ uses callable behavior
- Familiarity with closures from Chapter 7, especially the idea that a lambda can carry an outside variable in its backpack
- Familiarity with value semantics and reference semantics from Chapter 3, because query results can contain references to existing objects
- Familiarity with reachability from Chapter 4, because deferred queries can keep sources and captured variables alive

Why This Matters

LINQ looks calm. You write a query, give it a name, and move on. That surface can mislead you into thinking you already have the result. Most of the time, you do not. You have a description of work that will run later.

That delay is useful. Deferred execution lets you compose a recipe in pieces, avoid work nobody asked for, and keep filtering close to the final request. Queryable LINQ can also let another system, such as a database, do the heavy preparation before your process receives the results.

The same delay explains a long list of real bugs. A query sees items added after it was defined. A database query runs twice. A slow filter executes again during logging. A captured variable changes before the query finally runs. None of these are strange once you use the right model.

Treat deferred queries as live recipes.

This chapter sits directly on top of Chapter 6 and Chapter 7. Generic sequences provide the ingredients. Delegates and lambdas provide the cooking instructions. Closures explain why some recipes carry outside settings with them.

Core Analogy

A LINQ query is a recipe card.

Defining the query writes the recipe card. It does not cook the dish. Enumeration cooks from the recipe card by walking through the source and applying the recipe's instructions. Materialization packs the finished meal into a sealed container, giving you a stable result you can carry away. Queryable LINQ hands the recipe card to another kitchen, such as a database provider, and that kitchen decides how to prepare it.

The source sequence is the kitchen counter. The items in the sequence are ingredients. A filter is an instruction such as "serve only ingredients greater than one." A projection reshapes each ingredient before serving. Sorting controls the serving order. The final enumeration is the moment someone asks the kitchen to produce food.

This analogy has one clear limit. Real recipe cards do not usually change meaning when the pantry changes, but deferred LINQ often reads from a live source. In this chapter, that difference is the point. The recipe card is stable, but the counter it reads from can change before cooking begins.

Mental Model

Language Integrated Query, or LINQ, is not one single execution mechanism. It is a set of query-shaped operations that can target different worlds.

The first world is in-memory LINQ. Here, the source is an in-memory sequence, usually shaped as IEnumerable of T. IEnumerable of T means a typed sequence that can be asked for one item after another. The query stores a source and a chain of operations. Those operations often contain delegates created from lambdas. When enumeration begins, LINQ pulls items from the source and asks each operation what to do with each item.

No cooking happens when the recipe is written.

Many LINQ operations are sequence-producing operations. They take one recipe card and return another recipe card with more instructions written on it. Filtering, sorting, and projection usually work this way. They describe more work, but they do not necessarily perform it yet.

Other operations are terminal operations. They ask for an answer now. A loop triggers enumeration because it asks for items one by one. ToList and ToArray trigger execution because they materialize the results into concrete collections. Count asks how many items match. Any asks whether at least one item exists. First asks for the first matching item. Operations such as Sum and Max also force the sequence to be inspected so they can produce one answer.

That is the first execution boundary.

The second world is queryable LINQ. Here, the source is shaped as IQueryable of T. IQueryable of T means a typed query surface that stores an inspectable description of work for a provider. Instead of storing ordinary delegate calls for immediate local execution, the query is represented as an expression tree. An expression tree is data that describes the query so another system can inspect it.

Providers need expression trees because a local delegate is already executable behavior for your process. A database provider cannot look inside an arbitrary compiled delegate and reliably translate it into database work. It needs the recipe written as data, not as a private instruction whispered to your local cook.

Queryable LINQ is usually deferred too. The expression tree can grow as you add filters, sorting, and projections. Execution happens when enumeration, materialization, or a terminal operation forces the provider to act.

The provider boundary decides where the work runs. Before the boundary, filtering and sorting can happen in the other kitchen. After crossing into in-memory work, filtering and sorting happen in your process over objects already brought back.

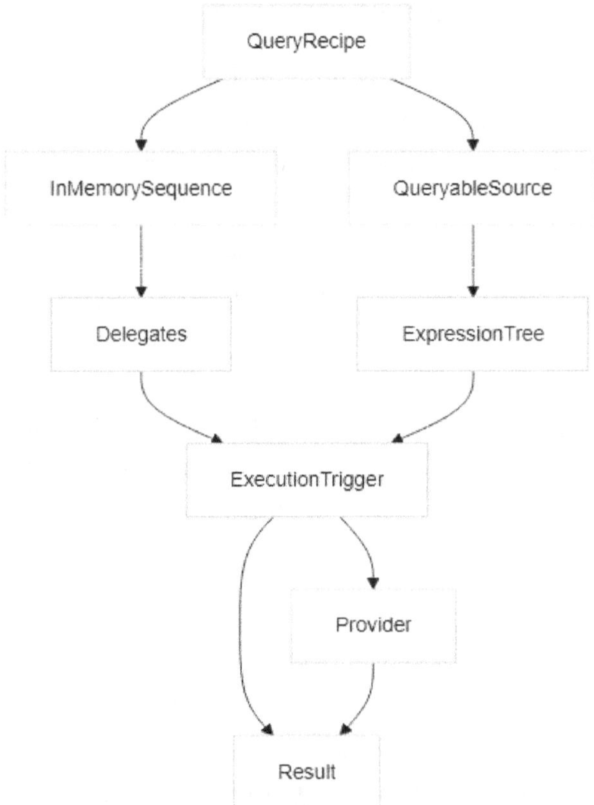

A common recognition cue is the declared shape of the source. If you are still working with IQueryable of T, the provider usually still has a chance to translate the recipe. If you materialize into a list or array, the provider part has already run. The remaining work is local. Calling a boundary operation that deliberately turns queryable work into enumerable work also moves the rest of the recipe into your process.

Here is a concrete boundary example. Imagine a database provider exposes invoices as IQueryable of T. If you add the overdue filter before materialization, the provider can translate that filter and return only overdue invoices. If you materialize first and then apply the overdue filter, you have already brought the earlier result set into memory. The later filtering happens on your kitchen counter, not in the database kitchen.

A thoughtful developer listens for that boundary.

Deferred execution means the query's result is delayed until enumeration or another execution trigger. Enumeration happens when something asks for the items one by one. That request can come from a loop, a materializing operation such as ToList or ToArray, or a terminal operation that must inspect the sequence to produce an answer.

Repeated enumeration means cooking the same recipe again. If the source changed, the second dish can differ from the first. If the source is expensive, the second pass can repeat the cost. If the source is queryable, the second pass can ask the provider to do the work again.

Materialization changes the situation. When you materialize, you force the query to run now and store the produced items in a concrete collection. The packed meal no longer asks the original recipe to cook again. It is a snapshot of what was served at that moment.

Materialize when stability matters.

Materialization has tradeoffs. It gives you a stable set of results, avoids repeated provider calls, and can make later decisions agree with each other. It also consumes memory, does work earlier than a deferred query would, and can become stale if the original source changes afterward. It does not deep-copy every object in the result. If the result contains reference objects, the collection is stable, but those objects can still be shared and mutable.

Closures add one more detail. A LINQ filter can use a variable from outside the query. As Chapter 7 explained, that variable rides in the closure backpack as a variable slot, not a frozen photo. If the outside variable changes before enumeration, the recipe reads the new setting when it cooks.

The backpack travels with the recipe.

Walkthrough

Start with a kitchen counter holding three ingredients labeled one, two, and three. You write a recipe card that says, "serve only ingredients greater than one." At this point, no one has cooked. You have a card with an instruction, not a plate of food.

The source is live. The counter still has the ingredients. The recipe card points to the counter and carries the filtering instruction, but it has not inspected the ingredients yet.

Now add a fourth ingredient to the counter. The recipe card already exists. Nothing about the written instruction changes. It still says, "serve only ingredients greater than one." The counter, however, now holds one, two, three, and four.

When someone finally asks the kitchen to cook from the recipe card, the recipe looks at the counter as it exists now. It examines one and rejects it. It examines two and serves it. It examines three and serves it. It examines four and serves it.

The served result is two, three, and four.

That outcome is the central lesson. The query looked at the counter when cooked, not when written. Defining the query did not freeze the ingredients. It preserved the recipe.

Now ask for the dish again. The kitchen does not replay a recording of the first plate. It follows the same recipe card again against the current counter. If the counter still holds one, two, three, and four, the result is again two, three, and four. If someone added five before the second request, the second result includes five as well.

Repeated enumeration repeats the cooking.

This is often exactly what you want. A live view can be useful when the source is changing and you intentionally want the latest answer. But it is wrong when you need a stable result for reporting, auditing, logging, or making two related decisions from the same data.

First extension: materialization. Imagine that before adding four, you ask the kitchen to cook the recipe and pack the finished meal into a sealed container. The packed meal contains two and three. After that, you add four to the counter. The container does not change. It is already packed.

That is what ToList or ToArray does conceptually. It forces the recipe to run at that moment and stores the result in a concrete collection. Later changes to the original source do not alter which items are in that materialized collection.

The collection is stable, not magical. If the materialized result contains references to existing mutable objects, the collection still points at those same objects. Chapter 3's shared online document link model still applies. Materialization freezes the membership of the result, not necessarily the internal state of every object inside it.

Second extension: queryable LINQ. The same recipe model explains queryable LINQ, but with another kitchen involved. Suppose the recipe card is not meant for your local counter. Instead, it is handed to a database provider. The provider reads the expression tree and decides how to translate the request. Filtering, sorting, and projection can happen in the database before objects come back to your process.

That can be excellent. It keeps large work near the data. It avoids carrying every ingredient across the room when the recipe only needs three of them.

The boundary matters. Once you cross from queryable work into in-memory work, the rest of the recipe runs locally. If the provider already narrowed the result, local work may be fine. If you crossed too early, you may have pulled a large amount of data into memory and then filtered it after the fact.

Do not cross the provider boundary by accident.

Third extension: closures. Picture the recipe card saying, "serve only ingredients greater than the current cutoff." The cutoff is an outside variable carried in the closure backpack from Chapter 7. The counter currently holds one, two, three, and four. If the cutoff is one when you write the recipe, then later becomes three before cooking, the recipe uses three at cooking time.

The exact result is four.

The recipe did not take a snapshot of the cutoff. It carried access to the variable slot. Deferred execution and captured variables combine, so the moment of execution controls both the source contents and the outside settings the recipe reads.

Once you see LINQ this way, many surprises stop being surprising. A query is a recipe card. Enumeration cooks. Materialization packs the meal for later use. Queryable LINQ lets another kitchen translate the card. The practical skill is knowing which moment you are dealing with.

Story or Scenario

A small billing team had a nightly job that reviewed customer accounts and sent a count of overdue invoices to an operations dashboard. The developer wrote a tidy LINQ query near the top of the method, then reused it twice. First, the job asked the query for a count of overdue invoices. That request triggered one enumeration. Later, after another step adjusted a few invoice statuses, the job asked the same query for overdue invoice identifiers for the log.

The count and the log disagreed.

Nothing was corrupt. The query was a recipe card, and the team had asked the kitchen to cook twice. Between the first and second enumeration, the counter changed. The second cooking used the new ingredients. During the billing review, I traced the disagreement to those two separate enumerations: one before the status adjustment, one after it.

The fix was not to make LINQ less lazy or to avoid LINQ entirely. The fix was to decide what the job meant. The dashboard needed one stable view of the invoices at the start of the billing pass, so the team materialized the query at that point and used the packed meal for both the count and the log.

The takeaway was plain: when two decisions must agree, cook once and keep the meal.

Common Misconceptions

- Defining a LINQ query executes it. This belief is tempting because the query expression reads like a complete request. The correct model is that most LINQ queries are recipes; they run when enumerated or when a terminal operation asks for an answer. Avoid the mistake by naming the first place where the recipe is cooked.
- A deferred query remembers the source as it was when the query was defined. This is tempting because a named query feels like a named result. The correct understanding is that the query usually reads the source later. Treat a deferred query over a mutable source as a live recipe.
- Enumerating the same query twice reuses the first result. This is wrong because deferred LINQ normally runs the recipe again. If the work is

expensive or the source can change, materialize once and reuse the materialized result.

- ToList and ToArray are just formatting choices. This belief is common because they often appear at the end of a query. They are execution boundaries that force cooking now and store a snapshot. Use them when you need stability, not as decoration.
- In-memory LINQ and queryable LINQ work the same way because the query syntax looks similar. This is wrong because in-memory LINQ runs delegates over objects, while queryable LINQ builds expression trees for a provider. Watch the provider boundary because it changes where the work happens.
- A captured variable inside a LINQ query keeps its original value. Chapter 7 already corrected this for closures, and LINQ does not change the rule. The query reads the captured variable slot when it runs. If the value must not change, create a separate stable value before the recipe cooks. In the backpack model, a stable value means a separate pocket whose contents you deliberately stop changing, not the same shared pocket with a different label.

Summary

LINQ is easiest to reason about when you treat a query as a recipe card. Defining the query writes the instructions, enumeration cooks the dish, and materialization packs the finished meal as a snapshot. In-memory LINQ cooks with delegates over objects. Queryable LINQ hands an expression tree to another kitchen, where a provider translates the work when execution is triggered. The essential habit is to locate the cooking moment. Once you know when the query runs and where it runs, you can predict whether it sees later changes, repeats work, or preserves a stable result.

Key Terms

- Language Integrated Query: Language Integrated Query, or LINQ, is the C# query model for describing filtering, shaping, sorting, grouping, and related sequence operations in a readable form.

- Deferred execution: Deferred execution means a query describes work now but performs the work later, usually when the query is enumerated or a terminal operation asks for a result.
- Enumeration: Enumeration is the act of asking a sequence for its items one at a time. For many LINQ queries, this is the cooking moment.
- Execution trigger: An execution trigger is an action that forces query work to run. Common triggers include looping through the sequence, materializing it, counting it, asking whether any item exists, asking for the first item, or converting it into another concrete result.
- Sequence-producing operation: A sequence-producing operation returns another recipe-like sequence and usually stays deferred. Filtering and shaping often behave this way until something asks for the items.
- Terminal operation: A terminal operation asks for an answer now instead of returning another deferred sequence. Counting, checking for any match, asking for one item, and materializing are common terminal operations.
- Materialization: Materialization forces a query to run and stores the produced results in a concrete collection. ToList and ToArray are common materialization operations. The collection membership becomes stable, but reference-type items inside it can still point to shared mutable objects.
- Stable snapshot: A stable snapshot is a saved result from a particular moment of query execution. It freezes which items were produced, not necessarily the internal state of shared objects those items reference.
- In-memory LINQ: In-memory LINQ runs over objects already in your process, commonly through IEnumerable of T. IEnumerable of T means a sequence that can be asked for items one at a time.
- Queryable LINQ: Queryable LINQ works through IQueryable of T. IQueryable of T means a query-shaped sequence that carries inspectable query data for a provider rather than only local callable behavior.
- Expression tree: An expression tree is a query represented as inspectable data rather than immediate callable behavior. Providers need expression trees because they can translate data-shaped

instructions, while ordinary delegates are local behavior they cannot reliably inspect.

- Provider: A provider is the component that receives a queryable recipe and decides how to execute it, often by translating it for a database or another external system.
- Projection: Projection is the query operation that shapes each item into a different form, like preparing each ingredient for serving.
- Provider boundary: The provider boundary is the point where work stops being translated by the query provider and starts running locally in your process. A common recognition cue is a conversion from queryable work to in-memory sequence work, after which later filtering or shaping happens in your application rather than in the provider.

Mini Quiz

1. **You define a LINQ query over a list, then add another matching item to the list before enumeration. What should you expect from a deferred query?**

   A. The new item is ignored because the query was already defined

   B. The new item appears because the query reads the source when enumerated

   C. The query fails because the source changed

   D. The query automatically materializes the original list

2. **What does materialization do in the recipe card model?**

   A. It writes a new recipe card but does not cook

   B. It hands the recipe to another kitchen

   C. It cooks now and stores the result as a stable snapshot

   D. It changes a delegate into an expression tree

3. **A team enumerates the same deferred query twice, and the second pass takes just as long as the first. What is the best explanation?**

   A. Deferred LINQ normally repeats the work each time it is enumerated

   B. LINQ always caches the first result automatically

   C. The runtime forgot the native machine code from the first pass

   D. The query became a record after the first enumeration

4. **Which statement best distinguishes in-memory LINQ from queryable LINQ?**

   A. In-memory LINQ always runs in the database, while queryable LINQ always runs in the application

   B. In-memory LINQ uses delegates over objects, while queryable LINQ builds expression trees for a provider

   C. In-memory LINQ cannot be deferred, while queryable LINQ is always eager

   D. In-memory LINQ requires records, while queryable LINQ requires classes

5. **A LINQ query uses an outside cutoff value, and that cutoff changes before enumeration. Which value does the query use?**

   A. The value from when the query was written

   B. The default value for the cutoff's type

   C. The value from when the project was compiled

   D. The current value in the captured variable slot when the query runs

6. **A query starts as provider-translated work, then the team converts it to an in-memory sequence before adding another filter. What should you recognize?**

   A. The later filter is now running locally in the application

   B. The provider still translates every later operation

   C. The query is no longer allowed to be enumerated

   D. The runtime automatically turns the filter into a database index

Answers are provided in the Answer Key at the end of the book.

Reflection Prompts

- Describe a query you've written that you assumed was already a result.
- Identify a place where two decisions in a program should use the same materialized snapshot.
- Compare a live deferred query with a materialized collection in one system you know.
- Recall a time when logging, counting, or debugging caused a query to run more than once.

Chapter 9: Async, Await, and Time

What You Will Learn

- Understand Task as a promise of future completion, not a dedicated thread
- Explain await as a pause point that records a continuation and returns control
- Describe why the compiler turns an async method into a state machine
- Predict why awaited work in a console app can resume on a different thread
- Connect synchronization context to continuation return rules
- Recognize why blocking on asynchronous work wastes threads and can deadlock
- Separate asynchronous waiting from parallel execution

Prerequisites

- Familiarity with the language promise, compiler behavior, and runtime behavior distinction from Chapter 1
- Familiarity with the Common Language Runtime execution model from Chapter 2
- Familiarity with delegates as callable values from Chapter 7
- Familiarity with closures as stored context from Chapter 7
- Familiarity with deferred work from Chapter 8, where work can be described now and performed later

Why This Matters

Async code is where many otherwise confident C# developers lose their mental footing. A method appears to pause, yet the application keeps responding. A Task appears in the type, and someone imagines a thread. A quick attempt to wait synchronously works in one small test, then deadlocks in a user interface application.

The danger is not that async is mysterious. The danger is using the wrong picture. If you picture a thread standing still, you write code that wastes capacity, blocks request handling, and traps continuations where they cannot resume.

This chapter gives you the correct picture: async is a continuation model over time. The compiler preserves your place, the runtime schedules the next part when the awaited operation completes, and no thread has to stand at the counter doing nothing.

Core Analogy

A Task is a restaurant pager.

You place an order at the counter. The restaurant gives you a pager. The pager is not the cook, and it is not the kitchen. It is a promise that your order will be ready later.

Await is the moment you hand over your pager number, step away from the counter, and let the restaurant continue serving other people. You are not occupying the counter while the kitchen works.

The continuation is what you plan to do when the pager buzzes. You return, pick up the order, and continue your meal from the place where you left off.

The synchronization context is the restaurant rule that decides where you should return when the pager buzzes, if such a rule has been captured. In a casual food hall, any pickup window may do. In a tightly managed restaurant, one specific counter handles your order, and you must return there.

Keep that picture. Task is the pager. Await leaves the counter. The continuation resumes when the pager buzzes. A captured synchronization context can control the return spot.

The analogy has one limit. A real pager holder stands around waiting and walks back on their own legs; in C#, the method's caller gets its thread back immediately, and the continuation may resume somewhere else entirely. The pager explains the waiting, not the return trip.

A Task is not a thread.

Mental Model

An async method is a method written so it can return control to its caller before all of its logical work has finished, then continue later after awaited work completes. Most async methods report that future completion with Task or Task of T. A non-generic Task represents completion without a result value. Task of T represents completion with a result value. Async void is reserved for event handlers because callers cannot await it in the normal way, and because a method returning no Task gives failures nothing to ride back on, so an exception there has nowhere to surface.

Start with the language promise. An async method can suspend at an await point and later continue as if the method had paused in place. Local state remains meaningful across the wait. Exceptions still travel through the method's logical flow. Failure and cancellation also flow through the Task, so the pager can report more than success.

Roslyn delivers that promise by changing the shape of the method. A state machine is a compiler-generated structure that keeps track of which part of the method should run next. It remembers where the method is, which local values must survive, what Task is being awaited, and what should happen after that Task completes.

That memory is the trick.

This connects directly to Chapter 7. A continuation is saved callable behavior, in this case, the rest of the async method. The compiler packages that continuation for you, so you get ordinary-looking control flow even though the method can stop and resume across time.

At runtime, await checks the pager. If the awaited Task is already complete, execution continues without leaving. If the Task is not complete, the state machine records the next step, arranges for that continuation to run later, and returns control to the caller.

No thread needs to wait during that gap.

The operation behind the Task may be a timer, network input and output, file input and output, or work already scheduled somewhere else. Often there is no active worker thread spending the whole wait doing your job. The Task represents eventual completion. It does not guarantee a private worker thread. Treat it as a promise, not a person.

A synchronization context adds a return-location rule when one is present and captured. Capture means the await records the current scheduling rule so the continuation can be posted back through that rule later. Some application models, especially user interface frameworks, use this so work that touches the visible user interface returns to the owning thread. Console and server applications generally do not have that kind of context. Their continuations still run, but they run without an original-thread guarantee.

On a payment callback service trace, I watched blocked request threads disappear once the team stopped synchronously waiting on Tasks that represented remote input and output. The work did not finish sooner, but the server stopped keeping workers idle while it waited for pagers to buzz.

Async is about not standing still during waiting. Parallelism is about simultaneous execution. They often appear near each other, but they are not the same idea.

Do not confuse waiting efficiently with working at the same time.

Walkthrough

You start an operation that takes 200 milliseconds. Picture yourself at a restaurant counter placing an order that will not be ready right away. The counter worker hands you a pager.

In C# terms, the operation gives you a Task. That Task says, “Completion will be known later.” It does not say, “A dedicated thread now belongs to you.” The pager is a promise, not the cook.

Your method reaches await. The compiler-generated state machine records where you are, keeps the local state needed later, and stores the continuation for the next part of the method.

Then your method steps away from the counter.

Control returns to the caller. The current thread is free to do other work. In a user interface application, that means the thread can keep processing input and repainting the screen. In a server application, the thread can go serve another request. In a console app, the thread is not consumed by a 200 millisecond nap just because the logical method is waiting.

The Task is still unfinished. The kitchen is still preparing the order, or the operation is waiting for time, input, output, or completion somewhere else. During that time, the state machine is quiet. It is not running slowly in the background. It resumes only when the pager buzzes.

When the 200 milliseconds pass, the operation completes. The stored continuation becomes ready to run.

Now the synchronization context matters. In a console app, there is usually no special rule saying, "Return to the exact same thread." If you printed the thread number before the wait and again after the wait, the second number may be different. The logical method continued, but the physical thread did not have to be the same one.

That outcome surprises developers who picture await as a thread pause. The better picture is restaurant pickup. You left the counter, and when the pager buzzed, the restaurant called you back. You are still the same customer with the same order. You are not proving that the same counter worker stood there motionless for 200 milliseconds.

A user interface application has another moving part: the user interface loop, often called a message pump. One thread repeatedly pulls work from a queue, such as mouse clicks, keyboard input, paint requests, and scheduled continuations. If that thread keeps looping, the application feels alive. If that thread stops, the screen freezes.

In a user interface app, the synchronization context usually says, "Continuations that started here should come back here." By default, an await in that context captures the rule. That rule exists because many user interface objects are only safe to touch from the thread that owns them. When the pager buzzes, you must return to the designated counter.

Blocking means forcing the current thread to wait synchronously instead of returning control to its normal work. A blocked user interface thread does not pump messages. It does not repaint. It does not run the continuation waiting in its queue.

This is where the trap closes.

The classic deadlock pattern follows directly from the pager model. A user interface thread starts async work, receives the pager, and then blocks while waiting for the result instead of awaiting it. The await inside the async operation has captured the user interface synchronization context by default. The continuation tries to return to the user interface thread because that is the captured return spot. But the user interface thread is occupied, standing at the counter, refusing to move until the continuation completes.

The continuation cannot run because the thread is blocked. The blocked thread cannot finish because the continuation cannot run.

That is the deadlock.

The cure is not to force the pager to buzz louder. The cure is to stop blocking the return spot. Await all the way up means each caller that can be asynchronous awaits the operation and returns control, rather than synchronously waiting for the result. This pattern continues up the call chain until you reach a true boundary, such as an event handler or framework entry point.

Treat this as the rule.

There is another practical lesson here. Async does not make a slow kitchen faster. If the operation takes 200 milliseconds because a remote service takes 200 milliseconds, async does not shrink that time by itself. It prevents your thread from being wasted during the wait. That is a capacity and responsiveness improvement, not magic speed.

For computation-heavy work, the picture changes. If you need to perform expensive calculations, something must actually do the computation. Async alone does not create extra cooks. Parallelism means arranging simultaneous execution. Async means not holding a worker hostage while waiting for time, input, output, or completion elsewhere.

I once reviewed a desktop import bug where every service call returned a Task, but the window still froze because the button handler synchronously waited for that Task. The team had bought pagers and then ordered everyone to stay at the counter.

Follow the pager and the behavior becomes predictable: order placed, pager received, counter left, pager buzzes, continuation resumes.

Story or Scenario

A small desktop team built an import button for a customer support tool. The import contacted a remote service, waited for a response, then updated the screen with the new cases. During testing, the developer noticed the screen froze while the import ran, so he changed the service call to return a Task.

The freeze remained.

The problem was not the Task. The problem was the waiting. The button handler started the asynchronous operation, then waited synchronously for the Task to complete. The pager existed, but the customer never left the counter. When the service response came back, the continuation needed the user interface thread so it could update the screen. That thread was still blocked, waiting for the continuation to finish.

The team fixed the handler by awaiting the operation instead of blocking on it. The button click returned control to the user interface loop. The screen kept repainting. When the pager buzzed, the continuation returned to the user interface thread and updated the list safely.

The insight was precise: async did not make the remote service faster. It stopped the user interface thread from standing still.

Common Misconceptions

- A Task is a thread. This belief is tempting because both Tasks and threads are associated with work happening later or elsewhere. The correct understanding is that a Task represents future completion; it does not promise a dedicated thread. Avoid the mistake by asking what completion the Task represents, not which thread it owns.
- Await blocks until the operation finishes. This belief comes from reading an async method as if it were ordinary step-by-step code. Await preserves the logical flow, but when the Task is incomplete, it records a continuation and returns control. Treat await as leaving the counter with a pager, not standing there until the food arrives.
- Async means parallel. This is wrong because waiting efficiently and executing simultaneously are separate ideas. Async helps when work involves time, input and output, or external completion. Parallelism

requires work to run at the same time. Keep the distinction clear: async frees the counter; parallelism adds cooks.

- The continuation always resumes on the same thread. This feels natural because the method's local variables are still there after await. The compiler preserves logical state, not physical thread identity. In a console app, resumption may happen on a different thread. In a user interface app, a captured synchronization context often sends the continuation back to the user interface thread.
- Blocking on async work is harmless if the result is needed. This is a dangerous habit. Blocking wastes a thread everywhere, and under a synchronization context it can deadlock by occupying the exact place where the continuation must resume. Treat awaiting all the way up as the rule unless a boundary absolutely forces synchronous behavior.
- Async methods run in the background automatically. This belief comes from seeing a method return before its work is complete. The method is not secretly running every line on a hidden worker. It runs until it reaches an incomplete await, stores the continuation, and resumes only when the awaited operation completes.

Summary

Async and await are best understood through the restaurant pager. A Task is the pager, a promise of future completion, failure, or cancellation. Await records where the method should resume, lets the current thread leave the counter, and arranges for the continuation to run when the pager buzzes. The compiler makes this possible with a state machine. A captured synchronization context can decide whether the continuation must return to a particular thread. The central rule is direct: async is not parallelism, and blocking on async work defeats the model. Let the pager do its job.

Key Terms

- Async method: An async method is a method written so its body can pause at await points and resume later. It usually returns a non-generic Task when there is no result value, or Task of T when it produces a result; async void is reserved for event handlers.

- Task: A non-generic Task is a promise of future completion with no result value. Task of T is a promise of future completion that carries a result value. Both forms can also represent failure or cancellation, and neither one is a dedicated thread.
- Await: Await is the language feature that observes a Task and, when the Task is not complete, records the rest of the method as a continuation. It lets the current thread return to other work instead of blocking.
- Capture: Capture means await records the current scheduling or return-location rule when one is present and capture is in effect. In a user interface application, that often means the continuation is posted back to the user interface thread.
- Continuation: A continuation is the remaining work that should run after an awaited operation completes. In async methods, Roslyn packages this continuation inside the compiler-generated state machine.
- State machine: A state machine is the compiler-generated structure that keeps track of where an async method paused and what it must remember. It stores the current point in the method, preserved local values, and the next action to perform.
- Synchronization context: A synchronization context is a scheduling rule that can control where continuations resume when it is captured. User interface frameworks commonly use one to return work to the user interface thread; console and server apps generally do not, so continuations still run but without an original-thread guarantee.
- User interface loop: A user interface loop, often called a message pump, is the loop that receives input, repaint requests, timer events, and other interface messages. If that loop is blocked, the application cannot process the continuation that needs to return there.
- User interface thread: A user interface thread is the thread that owns and updates visual interface objects in many desktop application models. Work that touches those objects often must return to that thread.
- Blocking: Blocking means keeping a thread stopped while it waits for an operation to finish. Blocking is different from awaiting because the thread cannot return to other work.

- Await all the way up: Await all the way up means letting each caller await the asynchronous work instead of forcing a synchronous wait in the middle. Treat it as the default rule because one blocked caller can trap the continuation that would finish the work.
- Deadlock: A deadlock is a waiting pattern where progress is impossible because each side is waiting for the other to move first. Blocking a user interface thread while a continuation needs that same captured thread is a classic async deadlock.
- Asynchronous work: Asynchronous work is work that allows a caller to stop waiting actively while completion happens later. The waiting often depends on outside completion, such as a timer, input, output, or a remote service, so it doesn't require a worker thread to stand idle.
- Parallel work: Parallel work is work performed by multiple workers at the same time. It is about simultaneous execution, not merely waiting without blocking.

Mini Quiz

1. **In the restaurant pager analogy, what does a Task represent?**

   A. The cook preparing the meal

   B. The counter worker taking orders

   C. The pager promising future completion

   D. The table where the customer sits

2. **What does await do when the awaited Task is not complete?**

   A. It blocks the current thread until the result is ready

   B. It forces the operation to finish immediately

   C. It creates a dedicated thread for the rest of the method

   D. It records a continuation and returns control

3. **A console app prints one thread number before an await and a different thread number after it. What is the best explanation?**

   A. The method restarted from the beginning

   B. The Task failed and retried automatically

   C. The logical method continued, but physical thread identity was not guaranteed

   D. The compiler skipped the continuation

4. **Why can blocking on async work deadlock in a user interface application?**

   A. The Task always requires two user interface threads

   B. The continuation may need the captured user interface thread that is blocked

   C. Await prevents the user interface from repainting

   D. The garbage collector pauses all continuations until blocking ends

5. **Which statement best distinguishes async from parallelism?**

   A. Async frees a thread during waiting; parallelism uses multiple workers at the same time

   B. Async means many workers compute at the same time; parallelism means waiting politely

C. Async only works in console apps; parallelism only works in user interface apps

D. Async and parallelism are the same runtime feature with different names

6. **A remote service takes 200 milliseconds to respond. What does async mainly improve in this situation?**

   A. It makes the remote service respond faster

   B. It removes the need for error handling

   C. It prevents a thread from being wasted during the wait

   D. It guarantees continuation on the original thread

Answers are provided in the Answer Key at the end of the book.

Reflection Prompts

- Describe a time when an application felt frozen while waiting for input, output, or a remote service.
- Identify a place in your own code where a Task represents waiting rather than active computation.
- Compare an async wait with work that benefits from simultaneous execution. Explain which one needs the pager model and which one needs more workers.
- Recall a user interface, server, or console situation where resuming on the original thread mattered, or did not matter.

Part IV: Safety and Judgment

Chapter 10: When Things Go Wrong: Exceptions and Failure Design

What You Will Learn

- Recognize exceptions as C#'s emergency failure channel, not a regular decision-making tool
- Distinguish invalid use, business refusals, and system failures
- Explain why guard clauses are usually the cheapest first defense for violated assumptions
- Reason about why the thrown exception path costs more than an ordinary check
- Describe stack unwinding as the runtime leaving the current path until it finds a matching handler
- Predict how exceptions inside Task-returning async methods travel through a Task and surface at await

Prerequisites

- The distinction from Chapter 1 between language promise, compiler behavior, and runtime behavior
- The execution model from Chapter 2, especially that runtime behavior has real cost
- The object lifetime model from Chapter 4, including that creating objects can add garbage collector pressure
- The type contract idea from Chapter 5, especially invariants and valid operations
- Helpful background from Chapter 7 on behavior stored now and invoked later, though this chapter leans most heavily on Chapter 9
- The Task, await, continuation, and async state machine model from Chapter 9

Why This Matters

Every useful program eventually faces a bad situation. A caller passes invalid information. A file is missing. A payment is declined. A remote service times out. A database connection fails halfway through work. C# gives you exceptions for failure, but that does not mean every negative answer belongs in an exception.

The mistake is treating all failures as the same kind of event. When teams do that, business refusals become expensive, noisy, and hard to reason about. A sold-out item is not the same as a broken oven. A missing required value is not the same as a network outage. Your design should tell those cases apart.

This chapter belongs here because you already have the runtime picture. You know that objects have cost, that runtime behavior matters, and that async work reports completion through a Task. Now we can add the missing judgment: how failure moves through the system, and which failures deserve the emergency channel.

Exceptions are alarms, not menu choices.

Core Analogy

Think of failure design as a restaurant service system.

The host stand is the boundary of an operation. The host checks whether an order is fit to enter the kitchen. If another employee hands the host an order card that violates the kitchen's rules, the host rejects it before cooking begins.

The kitchen is the operation doing the work. A finished meal is successful completion. The server carries the answer back to the customer or to the next station.

A business refusal is a service response. If the fish is sold out, the restaurant does not trigger the kitchen alarm. The server says the item is unavailable and gives the customer a clear way to choose what happens next.

An exception is the kitchen alarm. The alarm interrupts service because something has gone wrong that the current station cannot honestly handle through its usual steps.

A handler is a manager or station lead trained to respond to that category of alarm. A server who cannot repair a smoking oven steps aside until the alarm reaches someone with authority to decide.

An awaited Task is the restaurant pager from Chapter 9. You place the order, leave the counter, and return when the pager calls you back. If the meal is ready, you receive it. If the kitchen alarm happened while you were away, the pager brings you back to hear about the failure.

The analogy has one boundary. A real restaurant alarm is loud and visible to everyone. A C# exception travels through a specific call path, not through the entire process by default. Keep that limit in mind. The alarm follows the chain of responsibility.

Mental Model

An exception is the language and runtime channel for reporting that execution cannot continue along the current path. It is not a fancy return value. When code throws, it tells the runtime, "Stop walking this road. Find someone responsible for this failure."

The language promise is that the current flow is interrupted. Work after the throw does not continue in that method unless a suitable handler takes control. The runtime begins stack unwinding, which means it leaves the current method, then the caller, then that caller's caller, until it finds a handler that matches the failure category.

Handlers match by exception type. A handler written for a specific category accepts that category and compatible derived categories. A broader handler can catch more failures, but it also takes on more responsibility. Catch broadly only at boundaries that can make a broad decision, such as logging, translating to a safe user response, or shutting down a failed operation.

Cleanup regions still get their chance to run when the exception is observed and the stack unwinds normally, though nothing runs if the process itself dies abruptly. A cleanup region is a guaranteed cleanup step tied to a scope, commonly used for deterministic release from Chapter 4. It is where the program releases a non-memory resource, such as a file handle or connection, even when the work leaves through an exception. Cleanup is not the same as handling. Cleanup leaves the station tidy; handling decides what the alarm means.

Keep those roles separate.

Throwing has real work attached to it. The runtime creates or carries an exception object, records failure information, preserves useful diagnostic context, searches for a handler, and unwinds the call stack. The check that notices a bad condition is cheap. The thrown path is expensive. Compared with a branch that checks a condition and returns a planned result, throwing costs more and says something stronger.

Use checks for planned decisions.

A guard clause is an early check at the boundary of a method or operation. Its job is to protect assumptions. If a method requires a customer identifier, a valid amount, or an object that must not be null, the guard acts like the host checking the order card before the kitchen starts cooking. When an internal caller violates the method's contract, the guard often throws because the caller has used the operation incorrectly.

User-facing validation is different. If a customer submits an incomplete form, the missing value is often part of the product conversation. The caller needs outcome data it can show, group, translate, or attach to a field. Treating every form mistake as an exception confuses invalid internal use with customer input that needs guidance.

Guard clauses are especially important for preserving invariants from Chapter 5. A type that accepts invalid state and hopes to recover later is a type that has already lost control of its rulebook. The right time to reject invalid use is before invalid state spreads.

Expected outcomes need a different shape. Failure-as-data carries outcome information in the returned answer, such as whether the operation succeeded, why it did not, what the caller can show a user, and whether retrying makes sense. A declined payment, an unavailable seat, a validation message, or a search with no matching item can be part of the service exchange. The caller should not need emergency handling to learn that the business answer is no.

Unexpected failures belong to exceptions. Disk failures, corrupted state, broken assumptions, impossible states, and unavailable dependencies can be exceptional when they violate the operation's contract. If the contract says a remote service is optional and absence is a supported outcome, report that as data. If the contract says the operation cannot proceed without that service, the failure is an alarm.

Classify failure by the caller-callee contract.

If the caller broke a precondition, guard the boundary and usually throw. If the callee completed the request but the business answer is no, return outcome data. If the callee cannot complete its promised work because something outside the planned exchange failed, throw.

Async does not change the meaning of exceptions. It changes where you observe them. Inside an async method that returns a Task-like result, an exception becomes part of the Task's recorded outcome. The Task can complete successfully, be canceled, or fault with an exception. When you await that Task, the failure is raised at the await point in the same logical flow you learned in Chapter 9.

I once traced a faulted checkout Task that looked missing until the caller's await surfaced it with the original context.

That model describes Task-returning async methods. Async void is different and belongs only to event handlers, because it does not give the caller a Task to await or inspect. Without the pager, the caller has no ordinary place to observe completion.

The practical rule is direct: reject invalid use early, return business outcomes clearly, and throw for true surprises.

Walkthrough

A reservation service inside the restaurant prepares an order card for the kitchen. Another station hands the host an order card with no table number, even though every internal kitchen order must have one.

Nothing has been cooked yet. No chef has guessed. No server has carried a half-formed instruction across the room. The host refuses the order immediately because the restaurant's own process has violated its contract. This is a guard clause. It protects the kitchen's assumptions before expensive or confusing work begins.

In C# terms, the method boundary is the host stand. The operation has rules. If an internal caller violates those rules, the method should stop near the entrance and say so clearly. The early condition check is cheap. If the guard throws, the thrown path is more expensive, but the design is still correct because the caller broke the contract.

Guard early.

A different case starts at the dining room door. A customer writes a reservation request but leaves the party size blank. The host does not treat the customer as a broken restaurant system. The host returns a clear response: the party size is required.

That is user-facing validation. It resembles the host asking for missing information rather than sounding the kitchen alarm. The product needs data it can show to the customer. The answer may name the missing field, explain the problem, and let the customer fix it. This is not the same as an internal station sending the kitchen an invalid order after promising it was complete.

Now a complete order reaches the kitchen. The table number is present. The item name is valid. The kitchen checks the menu stock. The salmon is sold out.

A well-run restaurant does not pull the alarm for this. Sold-out food is disappointing, but it is part of service. The server returns with a polite refusal and offers alternatives. The customer can choose chicken, pick a later reservation, or leave.

That is failure-as-data. Failure-as-data means the operation returns a planned answer that says the requested outcome did not happen and gives the caller enough information to decide the next step. No stack unwinding is needed. No emergency manager has to run across the room. The design makes the negative answer visible without calling it a system failure.

This distinction matters most at boundaries where business rules live. A payment decline is usually not a broken payment system. A user name already being taken is usually not a server emergency. A search returning no records is often just an empty answer. Treat these as results the caller must inspect.

Later, the host checks another valid order. The item is available. The kitchen begins cooking. Halfway through, the oven shorts out and fills the kitchen with smoke.

Now the alarm is correct. The kitchen cannot finish the meal through its planned steps. The server cannot solve the electrical problem by offering fries. The cook cannot pretend the order succeeded. The current path is no longer safe, so the alarm interrupts service.

This is the role of an exception. Throwing says the current operation cannot complete according to its contract. The runtime stops walking the planned path and starts looking for a handler. That handler may be close, like a method that knows how to retry a temporary operation. It may be farther away, like an application boundary that logs the failure and returns a safe message to the user.

The alarm travels past workers who cannot fix it. A busser cannot repair the oven, a server cannot either, and a line cook cannot decide whether to close the kitchen, so the alarm keeps moving until it reaches the manager. In C#, frames without a matching handler do not observe the exception at all; the search passes through them and they cease.

That is stack unwinding. The current method exits because it cannot continue. Its caller exits if it also has no matching response. The runtime continues outward through the call chain. At each level, a handler either accepts responsibility or the unwinding continues.

Notice what this reveals. A handler is not just a place that notices failure. It is a place that can make a meaningful decision. It can retry the work, translate the failure into a different form for the next boundary, compensate by undoing related work that already happened, log at the correct boundary, release a resource, or present a safe response.

Responsibility is the test.

Handling, cleanup, and rethrowing are different actions. Handling means the station takes responsibility and chooses the next safe step. Cleanup means the station leaves its area safe before the alarm continues. Rethrowing means the station records or adds context, then lets the alarm keep traveling to someone better placed to decide.

Do not silence alarms you cannot handle.

A team then makes a bad restaurant policy. Every sold-out item now triggers the kitchen alarm. Salmon unavailable, alarm. Dessert finished for the night, alarm. A seasonal drink removed from the menu, alarm.

Service slows down. Managers keep running to business refusals. The staff becomes numb to alarms because most alarms are not emergencies. Real emergencies become harder to spot because the signal is polluted.

This is what happens when exceptions become control flow for planned outcomes. The program still works in the narrow sense, but the design lies about meaning. Business responses now look like system failures. Hot paths pay emergency costs. Logs fill with noise. Callers cannot tell whether they should choose another menu item or wake someone up.

The cost is not only speed. It is judgment.

Now connect this to async from Chapter 9. An order is placed and the customer receives a pager. The customer leaves the counter while the kitchen works. During that time, the oven fails.

The pager is not the cook. The pager is the promise that the order will eventually report an outcome. If the meal finishes, the pager brings the customer back for the meal. If the kitchen alarm happened, the failure is stored with the order. The customer learns about it when returning to the counter.

That is how exceptions travel through an awaited Task. The failure does not vanish because time passed. It does not require a thread to stand still. The async state machine records the continuation, and the Task records completion. When await observes a faulted Task, the exception is raised into your logical flow at the await point.

An unawaited Task is like a pager left on a bench. The kitchen may finish or fail, but the customer has walked away from the usual reporting point. In real programs, unobserved Task failures make errors harder to connect to the work that caused them. Treat fire-and-forget work as a design decision that needs an owner, logging, and a failure policy.

This is why async failure handling belongs near the await where the caller has context. The method that starts the work may be far away from the place that understands the user action, retry policy, or boundary response. Await brings the failure back to the point where the continuation resumes.

You revise the restaurant design.

Invalid internal orders are rejected at the host stand. Customer input problems are reported as validation responses. Business refusals, such as sold-out items, are returned as planned outcome data. True surprises, such as broken appliances, use the alarm. Pager orders report either ready meals or failures when the customer returns.

That is the model to carry into C#. Invalid use gets guarded. Expected business outcomes become data. Unexpected failures throw.

Story or Scenario

A small commerce team owned a checkout service that processed discount codes. The first version used exceptions for every rejected code. Expired code, exception. Code already used, exception. Code for a different region, exception. The service worked during testing because most sample checkouts used valid codes.

Then a holiday campaign started. Thousands of customers tried old codes from shared screenshots. The logs filled with stack traces for customer-visible rejections. Alerting became useless because the team could not tell a broken discount engine from ordinary shopper behavior. The kitchen alarm was ringing for every sold-out dessert.

On one checkout incident I reviewed, expired-coupon exceptions hid a real pricing-service outage for twenty minutes.

The team changed the boundary. Missing internal inputs were still rejected immediately by guards, because those were invalid orders inside the system. Customer-visible discount outcomes became answers the caller had to inspect, such as accepted, expired, already used, or not applicable. Exceptions remained for true surprises, such as the pricing service failing when pricing was required or the discount rules being unreadable.

After that change, support could explain refusals without treating them as incidents. Engineers could trust alarms again. The takeaway was not that exceptions are bad. The takeaway was that alarms must keep their meaning.

Common Misconceptions

- Exceptions are just another way to return a value. This belief is tempting because exceptions can carry information back to a caller. The corrected understanding is that exceptions interrupt flow and trigger stack unwinding. Avoid this mistake by reserving exceptions for paths where execution cannot honestly continue.
- Throwing is fine for expected failures if the code looks cleaner. This is common because exception-based code can hide decision branches. The corrected understanding is that hiding the branch does not remove the cost or the design signal. Treat planned business outcomes as data when the caller is supposed to respond.
- Guard clauses are defensive clutter. This belief appears when developers focus only on the happy path. The corrected understanding is that guards protect method assumptions near the boundary and prevent invalid state from spreading. Use guards where a method contract would otherwise be violated.
- Guard clauses and user validation are the same thing. This is wrong because an internal contract violation and an incomplete customer submission mean different things. Throw for invalid use of an operation; return validation data when the caller needs to help a user correct input.
- Catching an exception means the failure has been handled. This is wrong because catching only gives code a chance to respond. If the handler cannot retry, translate, compensate, release, report correctly, or rethrow with useful context, it has not handled the failure. Let the alarm continue to a boundary that can act.
- Async exceptions happen on some mysterious background thread. This is tempting because the failure is often observed later. The corrected understanding is that an exception inside a Task-returning async method is recorded by the Task and reappears when await observes that Task. Reason from the logical continuation, not from a fixed physical thread.
- All negative results should be exceptions so callers cannot ignore them. This overuses the emergency channel. The corrected understanding is that application programming interface shape should force attention

without lying about severity. Use explicit result data for planned business outcomes, and design the caller's path so ignoring that data is visibly wrong.

Summary

Failure design is about keeping signals honest. In the restaurant model, the host rejects invalid internal orders early, customer input problems become validation responses, sold-out items become business refusals, and the alarm is saved for real emergencies. C# exceptions are that alarm. They interrupt flow, unwind the stack, and search for a handler that matches the failure category and can respond. Use guard clauses to protect assumptions cheaply, even though the thrown guard path still has exception cost. Model planned outcomes as data when callers are meant to decide what comes next. Throw when the current path cannot continue safely. In async code, remember the pager: a Task records the failure, and await brings it back into your logical flow.

Key Terms

- Exception: The emergency failure channel in C# for reporting that execution cannot safely continue along the current path.
- Throw: The act of starting exception flow. Throwing interrupts the current path and asks the runtime to find a handler.
- Handler: Code that accepts responsibility for an exception. A real handler makes a meaningful decision, such as retrying, translating the failure into a safer message, compensating for partial work, logging at a boundary, or presenting a safe response. A catch that doesn't make such a decision has only silenced the alarm.
- Exception category: The kind of exception being reported, usually represented by its exception type. Handlers match against exception categories so the right response handles the right failure.
- Stack unwinding: The runtime process of leaving the current method and moving outward through callers until a matching handler is found.
- Cleanup region: A protected part of execution where cleanup is attempted as control leaves, whether the work finishes successfully or

an exception passes through. Cleanup regions support deterministic release for unmanaged resources and similar obligations.

- Guard clause: An early check that protects a method or operation from invalid use. Guard clauses often throw for internal contract violations, while customer-facing validation often returns outcome data the caller can show or inspect.
- Caller-callee contract: The agreement between a caller and an operation about what the caller must provide and what the operation promises to do. Classify a failure by this contract first: a valid negative answer belongs in outcome data, while a violated contract or broken promise belongs on the exception path.
- Expected outcome: A negative or alternate result that belongs to planned program flow because the caller is meant to inspect it and decide what happens next.
- Failure-as-data: A design choice where a planned problem is returned as information instead of being thrown as an exception. The returned information usually carries a status, a reason, and enough detail for the caller to decide the next step.
- Faulted Task: A Task that completed by recording an exception. Awaiting a faulted Task usually observes that failure in the logical flow, while exact wrapping and aggregation depend on how the Task is observed.
- Invalid use: A caller action that violates the contract of a method, type, or operation. Invalid use should be rejected close to where it enters.
- Unexpected failure: A failure that prevents the current path from safely continuing, such as corrupted state, a violated assumption, or an unavailable dependency that the operation contract required to be available.

Mini Quiz

1. **In the restaurant analogy, what does an exception represent?**

   A. A finished meal ready for the customer

   B. A sold-out menu item reported politely

   C. A kitchen alarm that interrupts service

   D. A table number written on an order card

2. **A caller asks whether a user name is available, and the answer is no because another user already owns it. Which design best matches the chapter's model?**

   A. Throw an exception every time the name is taken

   B. Return an outcome that says the name is unavailable

   C. Let the operation continue and fail later

   D. Block the calling thread until the name changes

3. **What does stack unwinding mean?**

   A. The runtime converts Intermediate Language into native machine code

   B. The garbage collector moves objects from Generation 0 to Generation 1

   C. The runtime leaves methods outward through the call chain while searching for a handler

   D. The compiler turns an async method into a state machine

4. **A private helper receives a value that its caller promised would already be valid. The value breaks that promise. What is the best match for this situation?**

   A. A guard clause should reject the contract violation early

   B. Customer-facing validation should always accept the value

   C. The garbage collector should clean up the invalid value

   D. The failure should be hidden and the operation should continue

5. **An exception occurs inside an async method that returns a Task. Where does the failure usually surface for the caller?**

   A. At the point where the Task is awaited

   B. Only on the original physical thread

C. Only when the garbage collector runs

D. At the moment the method is first named

6. **A team catches an exception, writes no meaningful response, and continues as if the operation succeeded. What is wrong with this design?**

   A. Catching is always slower than throwing

   B. The handler silenced the alarm without handling the failure

   C. The exception was converted into Intermediate Language

   D. The Task became a thread

Answers are provided in the Answer Key at the end of the book.

Reflection Prompts

- Describe a failure in one of your recent projects that should have been outcome data rather than an exception.
- Identify a method boundary where a guard clause would make the caller-callee contract clearer.
- Compare two negative outcomes in your domain, one that is a planned result and one that is truly exceptional.
- Recall an async failure you debugged, and explain where the exception was actually observed.

Chapter 11: Nullability, Patterns, and C# 14 Ergonomics

What You Will Learn

- Understand nullable reference types as compile-time annotations and warnings, not runtime enforcement
- Recognize where runtime null checks still matter, especially at boundaries and guard points
- Explain pattern matching as safe shape recognition rather than ordinary casting
- Reason about how patterns narrow values based on type, null-state, properties, positions, relationships, and list-like collection shape
- Understand how the field keyword keeps property validation close to the property surface
- Predict how null-conditional assignment behaves when the target is missing
- Recognize extension members in extension blocks as cleaner surfaces for existing types
- Treat C# 14 ergonomics as intent-sharpening tools, not substitutes for contracts and validation

Prerequisites

- Familiarity with value semantics and reference semantics from Chapter 3, especially why a reference can point to no object
- The working model of type contracts, records, interfaces, equality, and invariants from Chapter 5
- Background familiarity with delegates and lambdas from Chapter 7
- Familiarity with deferred execution from Chapter 8, especially the idea that captured variables and object state can be observed later

- The guard clause, caller-callee contract, and invalid use model from Chapter 10

Why This Matters

Null bugs survive because they hide in the gap between what you meant and what the runtime actually receives. You meant "this customer exists." The runtime receives a reference, and that reference either reaches an object or reaches nothing. That difference is not philosophical. It decides whether the next operation proceeds or fails.

Modern C# gives you several tools to narrow that gap. Nullable reference types let you write your intent into the type surface, and Roslyn objects when your flow looks unsafe. Runtime checks enforce the contract when real data arrives. Pattern matching lets you inspect shape before use. C# 14 also adds ergonomic features. Ergonomics here means language support that makes a correct intention easier to write, easier to read, and easier to place where a maintainer expects to find it.

Do not confuse clearer expression with guaranteed safety.

This chapter belongs after failure design because nullability is partly a contract topic. A nullable annotation tells the caller what you expect. A guard clause enforces what must be true. Pattern matching lets you prove a value has the shape you need before you rely on it.

Core Analogy

Think of an airport security checkpoint.

Nullable annotations are travel notes printed on the ticket. One note says the passenger should have identification. Another says identification may be missing. These notes help the check-in agent spot problems early, but they do not physically inspect the passenger.

Compiler warnings are the check-in agent's objections. The agent sees a ticket marked "identification may be missing" and says, "This passenger is being sent toward a lane that requires identification." That warning happens before boarding, while the travel plan is still being reviewed.

Runtime null checks are the actual identity inspection at the security desk. The officer looks at the passenger standing there now. If the required identification is missing, the officer stops the passenger. This is real behavior, not advice.

Pattern matching is routing passengers through the right lane based on what they actually carry and who they actually are. A passenger with a child stroller goes to one lane. A passenger with a premium ticket and one bag goes to another. A passenger carrying an oversized case gets redirected. The routing is based on observed shape.

C# 14 ergonomics are clearer counter procedures. The field keyword gives the property desk a clean way to check and update its stored value. Null-conditional assignment lets staff update a passenger record only if the record exists. Extension members in extension blocks add service counters for existing ticket types without rebuilding the airline system.

The airport notes reduce mistakes. They do not replace security.

Mental Model

Start with the reference itself. From Chapter 3, a reference is a link to an object. Null means there is no object at the end of that link. The language can help you talk about that possibility, but the runtime still sees a reference value.

Nullable reference types are a compile-time safety layer. They are annotations Roslyn uses while analyzing your program. When the flow says a reference may be null and your next action assumes an object exists, Roslyn warns you. The warning is useful because it points at a place where your intent and your evidence disagree.

Warnings are not walls.

At runtime, nullable annotations do not exist as active guards. They do not stop a caller from passing null. They do not automatically throw when a property receives null. If real enforcement matters, you write real checks at the boundary. That means constructor checks, method argument checks, property validation, and other guard points from Chapter 10.

Pattern matching adds a different kind of safety. It asks whether a value has a usable shape before you treat it as that shape. Narrowing is the compiler reducing what it still considers possible about a value after a successful check.

A value that was previously "some object, or possibly nothing" can become "a non-null passenger record" after the pattern supplies enough evidence.

That evidence comes in several forms. A type pattern checks whether the value is an instance of a particular type and, when it succeeds, makes that more specific type available. A property pattern checks named facts exposed by the value, such as a status, a destination, or a nested contact record. A positional pattern checks ordered parts exposed by the type, often through record-style or deconstruction-friendly shape. A relational pattern checks a value against a boundary, such as greater than a limit or less than a limit. It is not the pattern category for standalone equality. A list pattern checks the shape of a list-like collection, such as whether it has a certain arrangement of elements.

Each kind of pattern is a lane at the airport, and each lane has an entry rule. In C# itself, these lanes appear in two main homes: is patterns and switch expressions. An is pattern asks one shape question inline, the way a single agent checks whether one passenger fits one lane. A switch expression routes one value across several shape cases and produces a result, the way the routing board sends each passenger down whichever lane their observed shape matches.

When a pattern succeeds, the next step is safer because the value has been inspected. This is not the same as casting and hoping. It is also more expressive than a plain type test when your decision depends on properties, ordered parts, boundaries, or list-like collection shape. Pattern matching says, "prove the passenger fits this lane before sending them through."

C# 14's field keyword belongs at the property desk, but you need one piece of setup first. A property is the public surface that callers use to read or set a value. Its accessors are the read and write procedures behind that surface. An automatic property is the compact form where the compiler supplies the hidden storage for you. That hidden storage is the compiler-generated backing field.

Before C# 14, the clean automatic property and the validated property often pulled in different directions. If you needed validation, you commonly stopped using the compact automatic form and declared a separate backing field yourself. The field keyword names the compiler-generated backing field inside property accessors, which lets you keep validation close to the property without declaring a separate field just to say where the value lives. The keyword appeared in C# 13 only as a preview feature and reached general availability in C# 14. One sharp edge: if a type already has its own symbol named field, the keyword shadows it inside property accessors. To refer to your own symbol there, you write it with a leading at sign or qualify it through this.

Protect invariants at the doorway.

Null-conditional assignment starts with the null-conditional operator. That operator means "continue through this member access only if the receiver is not null." C# 14 extends that idea to assignment. Null-conditional assignment means "perform this update only if the target exists."

Ordinary assignment gives a target a new value. Compound assignment reads the current value, combines it with another value, and writes the result back as one assignment-shaped operation. C# 14 supports both ordinary assignment and compound assignment through the null-conditional form. It does not support increment or decrement through that form. Do not carry the mental model into those operations.

The skip behavior matters. If the passenger record exists, the update proceeds. For compound assignment, the current value is read, the combining work happens, and the result is written back. If the passenger record is null, the assignment is skipped. The member is not read or written, and the value that would have been assigned is not evaluated for that missing target.

On a notification service I helped diagnose, an optional loyalty-record update was only safe after we confirmed the skipped assignment did not hide a required audit side effect.

Extension members in extension blocks belong to the added service counters. The motivation is practical: sometimes you do not own a type, or you do not want to change its original contract, but you still want related helper behavior to appear near that type in a readable way. Extension blocks let you organize those external declarations together instead of scattering them as loose helper methods.

C# 14 includes extension properties and static extension members in that model. An extension property presents member-like read or computed behavior around an existing type. It does not add a field, private access, or per-instance storage. A static extension member attaches external behavior to the type-level surface rather than to one instance. Extension blocks organize declarations. They do not modify runtime identity, rewrite the original type, bypass access rules, or change the type contract from Chapter 5.

The original type remains the original type.

The through-line is intent. Nullable annotations state intent. Warnings challenge weak intent. Runtime checks enforce required intent. Pattern matching proves shape. C# 14 ergonomics make the intent easier to express in the place where readers expect to find it.

I once reviewed a production import failure where every editor warning was clean, but a partner feed still sent missing names through an unguarded boundary. The lesson was not that nullable annotations failed. The team had mistaken a ticket note for the security desk.

Walkthrough

A passenger arrives at the airport with a ticket marked "identification may be missing." In C# terms, you have a reference that may be null. The ticket note is not the same as an inspection. It tells the check-in agent to be cautious before sending the passenger into a lane that requires identification.

The check-in agent reviews the planned route. The passenger is headed to a security lane where identification is mandatory. The agent objects before boarding begins. That is the nullable reference type warning. Roslyn sees that your flow has not proven an object exists, and it warns that the next operation assumes too much.

Nothing has failed yet. The warning is preflight guidance.

Now the passenger reaches the security desk. The officer asks for identification. If the passenger has it, the line moves. If the passenger does not have it, the officer stops the passenger right there. That is the runtime null check. It is actual behavior during execution. It protects the boundary even if someone ignored the earlier warning, suppressed it, came from older code, or arrived through external data.

This is why annotations and guards work together. The annotation improves the route map. The guard protects the checkpoint. One prevents many mistakes during development. The other handles the world as it is during execution.

Next, the passenger moves toward routing. The airport does not route everyone by one vague label. Staff look at concrete facts. A passenger record says the traveler is an adult, the destination is international, the checked bag count is two, and the loyalty record is missing. Each fact can change the correct path.

Pattern matching works the same way. You do not merely ask whether a value exists. You ask whether it has the shape needed for the next action. A type pattern asks whether the passenger belongs to a certain category, such as a passenger record rather than a raw import row. A property pattern checks named facts, such as destination, contact status, or loyalty status. A positional pattern checks ordered parts exposed by the type, such as a pair of route values. A relational pattern checks whether a number falls above or below a boundary, such as whether the checked bag count is greater than the free allowance. A list pattern checks whether a list-like collection has the needed arrangement, such as a route with the expected first and final stops.

That is inspection, not optimism.

When the pattern succeeds, the route becomes safer. The value has been inspected. The compiler can often understand the narrowed type or null-state, so the next step is no longer guesswork. This is especially useful when your input comes from broad types, optional data, interface-based contracts, or mixed collections.

Pattern matching is inspection before trust.

The next group of C# 14 features serves a shared purpose. Each one helps place intent at the counter where a reader expects the rule to live. Property validation belongs near the property. Optional updates belong at the update point. External convenience behavior belongs near the type it helps, without pretending to be inside it.

Imagine a counter rule for updating a passenger's record. If the record exists, the agent adds a note. If the record is missing, the agent does nothing. The absence of a record is not treated as an emergency; it is treated as "there is nowhere to write." That is null-conditional assignment.

Make it concrete. A customer variable is null, and the code uses null-conditional assignment to give that customer an order. Predict the outcome before reading on. The observed result: nothing happens, and the right side, the order, is never even evaluated. Now the customer exists, and the same assignment runs again. This time the order is evaluated and the assignment lands.

The exact prediction is specific. When the target exists, the assignment happens. If the assignment uses a value that must be computed, that value is computed as part of the update. When the target is null, the update is skipped. The missing member is not read, the missing member is not written, and the would-be assigned value is not evaluated for that missing target. For compound assignment, the same conditional idea applies when the target exists: read, combine, and write. For increment and decrement, C# 14 does not support the null-conditional form.

Do not generalize beyond the feature.

Move to the property desk. The airline stores each passenger's display name, but the name has an invariant. It cannot be empty after trimming, or perhaps it must fit a length rule. The property is the desk customers interact with. The stored value is behind the counter.

With the field keyword inside property accessors, the property desk can inspect the incoming value and update the compiler-generated storage directly. The validation remains beside the property surface where readers expect it. You do not need to scatter the rule by introducing a separately named backing field unless the design genuinely needs one. The result is not a new kind of safety. It is a cleaner location for an old responsibility.

The airport adds one more service. Frequent travelers use an existing ticket type, but the airline wants a cleaner way to expose extra conveniences around it. The airline cannot rebuild every ticket already issued, and it should not pretend those tickets have private internals they do not expose. So it opens an added service counter beside the normal counters.

That is the role of extension members in extension blocks. They let you present external behavior as a cleaner grouped surface for existing types. Extension properties make read-like or computed facts feel natural, but they do not add storage to each ticket. Static extension members attach behavior to the ticket type's public-facing surface rather than to one passenger's ticket. The original type remains the original type. The extension surface is still outside it.

A good developer reads these features as counter procedures, not as security replacements. Nullable annotations reduce confusion. Runtime checks enforce boundaries. Pattern matching routes safely based on observed shape. The field keyword, null-conditional assignment, and extension blocks make common intentions clearer.

Ergonomics do not replace judgment.

Story or Scenario

A team maintains a booking service for a regional airline. The service has grown for three years, and its passenger records arrive from several places: the public site, a partner portal, and a nightly import. The codebase uses nullable reference types, so the editors show warnings when a passenger contact may be missing. For months, developers treat those warnings as if they are enough.

Then a partner import sends several records with missing contact names. The internal model says the name should not be null, but the import path bypasses the usual screen validation. A late-night job fails halfway through, leaving support staff with a partial passenger list and no clear explanation for several skipped notifications.

The fix is not to abandon nullable annotations. The team keeps them. They also add boundary guards where external data enters, move property validation closer to the property surface using the field keyword, and replace several fragile casts with pattern matching that checks record shape before routing passengers through notification rules. One optional update becomes a null-conditional assignment because absence of a loyalty record is acceptable.

The lesson is plain: ticket notes help staff plan, but the security desk still has to check the person standing there.

Common Misconceptions

- Nullable reference types prevent null at runtime. This belief is tempting because warnings feel like enforcement in modern editors. The correct understanding is that nullable annotations guide Roslyn at compile time; they do not create runtime checks. Keep real guards at boundaries where invalid null values must be rejected.
- A clean nullable warning list means the program is null-safe. This is wrong because warnings only cover what the compiler can analyze and

what annotations accurately express. External data, older libraries, reflection-based paths, suppression, and incorrect annotations still exist. Treat a clean warning list as a strong signal, not a proof of safety.

- Runtime null checks are redundant when annotations are present. This belief comes from confusing the ticket note with the identity inspection. Guards are still required when the caller-callee contract must be enforced during execution. Put guards where bad input crosses a trust boundary or would corrupt an invariant.
- Pattern matching is just nicer casting or a longer way to write a type test. This is too small a view. A cast tries to treat a value as a target shape and fails if that hope is wrong. A plain type test answers only one category question. Pattern matching can inspect type, null-state, named properties, ordered parts, boundary relationships, and list-like collection shape before the next step relies on them.
- The field keyword changes the meaning of properties. It does not change the property contract by itself. It gives accessors a clean name for the compiler-generated backing field so validation and storage can live close together. Use it to protect invariants at the property surface, not to hide complex behavior inside surprising accessors.
- Null-conditional assignment is the same as always assigning a value. This is wrong because the assignment is skipped when the target is null. The useful mental model is “update the record only if the record exists.” Remember that C# 14 supports ordinary assignment and compound assignment in this style, but not increment or decrement.
- Extension members change the original type. They do not. Extension members in extension blocks add an external surface that can read like part of the type, but they do not rewrite the type, bypass its access rules, add fields, create per-instance storage, or alter its identity. Use them to organize helpful behavior around existing types without pretending you own the original contract.

Summary

Nullability, pattern matching, and C# 14 ergonomics all help you express safer intent, but they operate at different points in the airport. Nullable annotations are ticket notes. Compiler warnings are the check-in agent’s objections.

Runtime null checks are the actual security inspection. Pattern matching routes passengers based on observed shape and can narrow type and null-state after inspection. The field keyword, null-conditional assignment, and extension members in extension blocks are clearer counter procedures that reduce mistakes without changing the original security rules. Use each tool for its proper job, and don't mistake a clearer route map for a locked gate.

Key Terms

- Nullable reference types: Compile-time annotations that describe whether a reference is expected to hold an object or may be null. Roslyn uses them to produce warnings; they do not enforce behavior at runtime.
- Compiler warning: A compile-time objection from Roslyn that points to code whose flow looks unsafe or inconsistent with its annotations. A warning is guidance, not a runtime barrier.
- Runtime null check: An actual execution-time check that rejects a null reference when the contract requires an object. Use it at boundaries, guard points, and invariant-protecting surfaces.
- Narrowing: The compiler's improved understanding of a value after a successful check. A successful pattern can narrow both the value's type and its null-state.
- Pattern matching: A C# feature for checking whether a value has a particular shape before using it that way. Patterns combine testing with narrowing, so the compiler can treat a successful value more precisely afterward.
- Type pattern: A pattern that checks whether a value is of a specific type. It is useful when input arrives through a broad contract or mixed source.
- Property pattern: A pattern that checks named properties on a value. It routes based on observed facts, not just on the value's broad type.
- Positional pattern: A pattern that checks ordered parts exposed by a type, often with records or deconstruction-friendly types. It fits values whose meaning is naturally expressed as a small set of ordered pieces.

- Relational pattern: A pattern that compares a value against an ordered boundary, such as being greater than or less than a meaningful threshold. Standalone equality belongs to other pattern forms, not to relational patterns.
- List pattern: A pattern that checks the list-like collection shape of a value. It can express expectations about length, position, or arrangement.
- Automatic property: A property whose storage is supplied by the compiler rather than written as a separate field by the developer. It gives the type a clean property surface while Roslyn handles the backing storage.
- Accessor: The get or set part of a property. Accessors define what happens when callers read from or write to the property.
- Compiler-generated backing field: The hidden storage Roslyn creates for an automatic property. Callers do not see it directly.
- The field keyword: A C# 14 feature that names the compiler-generated backing field inside property accessors. It helps keep validation and storage close to the property surface without exposing the field to callers.
- Null-conditional operator: An operator that continues through a member access only when the target exists. If the target is null, the access stops instead of dereferencing a missing object.
- Compound assignment: An assignment form that combines an operation with storing the result back into the same target. It is still an assignment, but it is not the same as increment or decrement.
- Null-conditional assignment: A C# 14 feature that performs ordinary assignment or compound assignment through the null-conditional operator only when the target exists. If the target is null, the assignment is skipped; increment and decrement are not supported.
- Extension members in extension blocks: A C# 14 feature for grouping extension behavior around existing types, including extension properties and static extension members. The original type is not changed, and extension members don't add fields, private access, runtime identity, or per-instance storage.

- Extension property: An extension member that offers property-like syntax around behavior associated with an existing type. It does not store new data inside each instance.
- Static extension member: An extension member called from the type-level surface rather than from an instance. It groups related external behavior near the type without changing the type's actual contract.

Mini Quiz

1. **What is the best mental model for nullable reference type annotations?**

   A. Runtime guards that reject null automatically

   B. Pattern rules that inspect object shape at runtime

   C. Special object wrappers that carry null-checking behavior

   D. Ticket notes that help Roslyn spot risky routes before execution

2. **A service receives customer data from an external partner. The model uses nullable annotations and the editor shows no warnings. What should the team still do at the boundary?**

   A. Trust the annotations and skip validation

   B. Add runtime guards for values required by the contract

   C. Replace all references with value types

   D. Disable nullable warnings for imported records

3. **A value arrives as a broad message type, and you route premium orders by checking that the message is an order, that its customer level is premium, and that the total is greater than a threshold. What does pattern matching add beyond a cast?**

   A. It tests observed shape and can narrow type and null-state after success

   B. It creates a new object with the requested shape

   C. It prevents all possible null failures at runtime

   D. It changes the original type's private fields

4. **What does null-conditional assignment do when the target is null?**

   A. It evaluates the target as missing and skips the assignment

   B. It creates the missing target and then assigns the value

   C. It performs increment or decrement anyway

   D. It retries the assignment through a runtime helper

5. **What is the purpose of the field keyword in C# 14 property accessors?**

A. To expose private storage to callers

B. To name the compiler-generated backing field inside the accessor

C. To make every property immutable

D. To replace the need for constructor guards

6. **What is true of extension members in extension blocks?**

   A. They add an external member-like surface around an existing type

   B. They add private fields to each existing instance

   C. They make nullable annotations enforce runtime checks

   D. They change the runtime identity of the original type

Answers are provided in the Answer Key at the end of the book.

Reflection Prompts

- Identify a place in your current or recent code where a nullable annotation communicates intent but a runtime guard still belongs.
- Describe a domain value, such as an order, message, claim, or payment, where type, property, positional, relational, or list patterns would make routing clearer.
- Compare a property in your own codebase with the airport property desk model. Where should validation live, and what storage should callers never see?
- Recall an optional update in an application you have worked on. Would null-conditional assignment express the intended behavior clearly, or would an explicit guard read better?
- Identify a helper behavior you have placed far from the type it describes. Would an extension block make that intent easier to find without pretending to modify the original type?

Chapter 12: Collections, Spans, and Performance Instincts

What You Will Learn

- Understand why lists grow in useful but costly steps
- Recognize how capacity affects copying and allocation in hot paths
- Explain how dictionaries use GetHashCode and Equals together
- Predict why mutating a dictionary key after insertion breaks lookup
- Distinguish copying data from viewing existing data through Span of T, ReadOnlySpan of T, or ReadOnlySpan of char
- Choose between Span of T and Memory of T based on lifetime needs
- Reason about first-run timing, warm-up, garbage collector pressure, and automatic .NET 10 runtime improvements

Prerequisites

- Familiarity with just-in-time compilation, tiered just-in-time compilation, dynamic profile-guided optimization, hot paths, cold code, and warm-up from Chapter 2
- Familiarity with value semantics, reference semantics, shallow copies, arrays as reference types, immutable strings, and the light introduction to spans from Chapter 3
- Familiarity with the managed heap, Generation 0, promotion, the Large Object Heap, and garbage collector pressure from Chapter 4
- Familiarity with type contracts, Equals, GetHashCode, records, classes, structs, and invariants from Chapter 5
- Familiarity with generics as real runtime types from Chapter 6
- Familiarity with deferred execution and materialization from Chapter 8

Why This Matters

Most C# performance problems in ordinary application code are not exotic. They come from growing collections repeatedly, copying data when a view would do, allocating temporary objects in high volume, measuring cold code, or breaking equality contracts that collections depend on. These are everyday mistakes, not advanced runtime mysteries.

Earlier chapters gave you the parts. Chapter 2 explained warm-up and just-in-time compilation. Chapter 4 explained garbage collector pressure. Chapter 5 explained equality contracts. Now those ideas meet collections and spans, where small choices repeat thousands or millions of times.

Performance is not guesswork. Treat it as accounting.

Core Analogy

Think of memory and collections as a bookshelf.

A list is a shelf that holds books in order. When the shelf fills up and more books arrive, the library staff may bring in a larger shelf and copy the existing shelf slots into the new one. In real life you move books. In C#, the list copies element slots. For reference-type elements, those slots hold links to objects, so the objects themselves are not duplicated. For value-type elements, the values are copied.

A dictionary is a labeled shelf index beside the bookshelf. GetHashCode chooses the shelf label where a key should be filed. Equals performs the final check once the index has found the right neighborhood. The label narrows the search; the equality rule confirms the exact book.

A span is a cardboard window laid over one continuous run of books. Continuous matters. The visible books sit next to each other with no gaps, just as contiguous memory means a run of elements laid out one after another. The books do not move. The window has a starting position and a length. Looking through the window lets you work with part of the shelf without copying that part onto a new shelf.

That distinction pays rent.

The window also has a strict lifetime. A Span of T is a current-method window over mutable contiguous storage. You do not store it on a long-lived object, and you do not carry it across an await point. ReadOnlySpan of T is the same kind of short-lived window with a rule that you cannot mutate through that view. For string data, the common view is ReadOnlySpan of char, because strings are immutable and should be inspected without pretending they are mutable.

Memory of T is a longer-lived window tag. You use it when a view-like relationship must be stored, passed around more freely, or carried across asynchronous boundaries. When you actually need to work with the data in a non-paused stretch of execution, you use an appropriate short-lived span view from that longer-lived representation.

Performance judgment is knowing whether you are expanding a shelf, rebuilding an index, copying books, or just looking through a window.

Copying is a choice.

Mental Model

A collection is not just a convenient shape around data. It is a set of promises with costs attached.

A list gives you ordered storage with fast access by position. Its internal storage has a current size and a capacity. Size is how many items you are using. Capacity is how many items the current shelf can hold before expansion. When you add beyond capacity, the list must acquire more room and copy existing element slots into that room. That movement is not a bug. It is how the shelf keeps the promise that items remain in order and can be reached efficiently.

Capacity matters most when growth happens on a hot path. If a list grows once during setup, you rarely care. If it grows inside a frequently repeated operation, each expansion becomes part of the bill. Planning capacity is useful when the size is predictable, but excessive unused capacity also costs memory. The instinct is not to make every shelf enormous. The instinct is to stop predictable shelf replacement where it repeats.

A dictionary makes a different trade. It gives fast lookup by key when the key's equality contract is stable. GetHashCode assigns a broad shelf label. Equals confirms the exact match among candidates under that label. Both are required. A hash code alone is not identity, because different keys can land under the same label. Equals alone is too slow for large shelves, because it would require checking too many books one by one.

Do not mutate dictionary keys.

That rule is not superstition. A dictionary files a key according to the key's hash and equality behavior at insertion time. If the key later changes in a way that changes GetHashCode, lookup walks to the wrong shelf label. If the key changes in a way that changes Equals but leaves the hash the same, lookup can reach the right neighborhood and still fail the final confirmation, or worse, confirm the wrong relationship. Either way, the index no longer describes the shelf honestly.

Spans solve a different problem. Contiguous memory means the elements sit in one uninterrupted run, so a view can describe them with a start and a length. Span of T is a stack-only window over mutable contiguous storage, such as part of an array. ReadOnlySpan of T is the read-only version for general element types. ReadOnlySpan of char is the natural view for string data, because the view can inspect characters without copying and without allowing mutation through the view.

The key idea is not where the books live. The key idea is that the window does not own the books.

ReadOnlySpan of T prevents mutation through that specific window. It does not make the underlying storage deeply immutable. If the same array is reachable through another valid mutable route, that route can still change the books. The read-only rule describes what this view can do, not what every other reference in the program can do.

C# 14 made array-to-span conversions first class. The language now treats the movement from an array to a span more naturally, so the window model fits more cleanly into ordinary C# expression. It reduces friction. It does not change what a span means. You are still viewing existing storage, not creating a new shelf.

Span of T has strict lifetime rules because it is stack-only. You do not store it in a class field. You do not carry it across an await point. You do not let it outlive the immediate area where the compiler can prove it is safe. Memory of T exists for the cases where the view must survive beyond those limits. It is the heap-safe counterpart. When you need a view-like reference that can be stored or kept across asynchronous work, Memory of T is the right shelf tag. During the active, non-paused processing step, a short-lived span can be used where the rules allow.

Lifetime decides the tool.

Performance instincts connect these pieces. Allocations feed the garbage collector. Short-lived allocations often disappear cheaply in Generation 0, but high volume still creates pressure. Large allocations can land on the Large Object Heap. Repeated copying burns time and memory bandwidth.

First-run measurements also include more than your own logic. They can include just-in-time compilation, tiered just-in-time compilation, and dynamic profile-guided optimization while the runtime learns which paths are hot. A warmed hot path can look different from a cold first run.

.NET 10 adds more automatic help, and the names are worth translating. Escape analysis means the runtime proves that an object never leaves the current method, so it does not need a managed heap allocation in some cases. Devirtualization means the runtime replaces an interface or virtual call with a direct call when it proves the concrete target. Inlining means the runtime folds a small called operation into its caller so the call overhead and extra indirection can disappear. Interface calls are calls made through a role contract rather than directly through a concrete type. Arm64 means the 64-bit Advanced RISC Machine architecture, common on modern servers, laptops, and mobile-class hardware.

The runtime is doing accounting too.

With those meanings in place, the .NET 10 news is easier to judge. Escape analysis can avoid heap allocation for some objects that never leave a method, including some delegates and enumerators. Some interface calls over arrays can be devirtualized and inlined when the runtime proves the concrete target. Garbage collection pauses on Arm64 improved; benchmarks showed pause improvements from roughly eight percent to over twenty percent. These are runtime wins, not excuses for careless shelves.

Good code gives the runtime fewer messes to clean up.

Walkthrough

Start with a small list on the bookshelf. In this teaching example, it has room for four books. Four is not a rule to memorize; it is just a small number that lets you hear the expansion happen. You place book one, book two, book three, and book four on the shelf. The shelf had enough room, and each new book slid into the next open position.

Then you add book five. The shelf is full, so the library staff brings a larger shelf. The list copies its existing element slots into the larger storage area, then places book five after them. If those elements are references, the copied slots point to the same objects as before. If those elements are values, the values are copied. Your list still behaves like one ordered collection, but internally the shelf changed.

Growth is useful, but it is not free.

Suppose you knew from the beginning that twelve books were coming. If you prepared a shelf with enough capacity, the staff would not need to interrupt the work to replace the shelf partway through. Capacity is not about changing the meaning of the list. It is about avoiding predictable expansion when you already know the size of the job. Do not turn that into a habit of oversized shelves. Extra capacity reserves memory whether you use it or not.

The same principle applies when a list sits inside a hot path. If you build a temporary list once during application startup, shelf expansion is probably noise. If you build the same growing list for every request, every frame, every message, or every row in a large batch, the cost repeats. At that point the shelf's growth pattern matters.

Next, place a dictionary index beside the shelf. You want to find books by a key, not by walking the whole shelf. The key might be a customer identifier, a product code, or a record-like value that represents several facts together. The dictionary asks GetHashCode for a shelf label. That label sends the lookup to a smaller neighborhood. Then the dictionary uses Equals to confirm which exact key in that neighborhood matches.

Both steps matter. If two different keys receive the same shelf label, the dictionary still works because Equals separates them. If two equal keys report different shelf labels, the dictionary is misled before Equals gets a fair chance. The label must be consistent with the equality rule.

Picture a mutable class instance representing a library card. This example uses a reference-type object on purpose, so the same object can be changed after insertion. When you insert it, the card says its branch is North and its number is 123. GetHashCode assigns it to the North 123 label area, and the dictionary files it there. Later, you change the same card object so its branch is West while it is still being used as a key.

The physical card is still somewhere in the index. But lookup now asks the changed card for its current label, and the current label points toward West 123. The dictionary looks in the West neighborhood. The card was filed under North. Lookup fails because the hash-based shelf label changed.

A second failure is quieter. Suppose the label stays the same, but a fact used by Equals changes. The dictionary reaches the old neighborhood, then asks for final confirmation. The changed key no longer compares the way it did when filed. Lookup can fail at the confirmation step. Hash stability and equality stability both matter.

This feels strange only if you forget the bookshelf index. The dictionary does not scan every shelf label on every lookup. That would defeat its purpose. It trusts the key's stable filing behavior.

Now return to a five-item array on the shelf. The items are one, two, three, four, and five. You want to work with the middle three items: two, three, and four. The old habit is to copy those three books onto a new small shelf. That gives you a separate collection, but it allocates new storage and copies data.

A span uses the cardboard window instead. You lay the window over the middle three books. The window records a start and a length. It does not move book two. It does not duplicate book three. It does not allocate a new array for book four. When you sum what you see through the window, you read the existing shelf.

The exact outcome matters. A span over the middle three of five array elements is a window, a start and a length over existing memory. Summing through it allocates nothing. Copying a sub-array creates another shelf and copies the visible books onto it.

Copying is still the correct choice when you need ownership. If the selected books must survive after the original shelf can change, if another component needs an independent snapshot, if you must send the data somewhere that stores it for later, or if concurrent changes would make a live view unsafe, copy the data. A span is best when the work is immediate and the source storage remains valid for the whole operation.

Do not borrow when you need ownership.

The window is not magic storage. It is a safe view. If the underlying array contents change while the span is still valid, the span sees those changed contents because the books are the same books. This follows the reference and sharing lessons from Chapter 3. The span did not take a photograph. It looks at the shelf.

ReadOnlySpan of T adds a reading-room rule. You can look through the cardboard window, but you cannot use that window to rearrange the visible books. Other valid mutable access to the same shelf can still rearrange them. For string data, ReadOnlySpan of char gives you a view over characters without copying and without pretending that the immutable string can be changed.

Memory of T changes the lifetime story. Span of T is stack-only, so it stays within a narrow, compiler-checked area. If you need to store the view in an object, keep it for later, or carry it through asynchronous work, the stack-only window is the wrong tool. Memory of T is the heap-safe way to represent a window-like relationship that must outlive the immediate stack frame. Across an await point, keep the Memory of T, not the Span of T.

This is where the bookshelf analogy has a limit. A cardboard window in real life can be left on a shelf all day. Span of T cannot. Its safety comes from strict lifetime rules enforced by the language and runtime design. Memory of T exists because real programs sometimes need a longer-lived handle to a region without pretending that a stack-only span can survive anywhere.

C# 14 makes array-to-span conversions feel more natural in the language. You can think of an array as a shelf that can readily receive a window. The language now treats that window placement as a first-class move, which reduces friction around a performance model that developers were already using. The span still means a view over existing storage.

Close the walkthrough by timing the shelf work. If you measure the first time the operation runs, you are measuring more than the bookshelf activity. From Chapter 2, you know the Common Language Runtime may still be translating Intermediate Language into native machine code. Tiered just-in-time compilation may start with a quick translation and later replace hot paths with better native code. Dynamic profile-guided optimization may use real execution behavior to improve the passages the program keeps rereading.

A cold timing includes translation and early learning. A warmed timing is closer to steady work.

Allocations also change the story. Copying sub-arrays creates new shelves. Growing lists creates replacement storage. Temporary objects increase managed heap activity. The garbage collector is very good at cleaning short-lived objects, but repeated temporary shelves still create work. If the same allocations happen inside hot paths, they become part of the system's rhythm.

On a reconciliation trace, I once watched temporary array slices dominate allocation samples while the database sat mostly idle.

.NET 10 helps when it can prove safety. Escape analysis can keep some short-lived objects off the managed heap when they never leave a method. That helps the bookshelf because some temporary helper objects never become shelves the garbage collector has to revisit.

Devirtualization and inlining help a different part of the work. When the runtime proves that an interface call over an array has a concrete target, it can replace the indirect call with a direct one and sometimes fold the called work into the caller. The shelf work becomes less indirect.

Garbage collection pauses on Arm64 improved, which helps applications running on that architecture. You do not write special ceremony to receive these benefits. You write clear idiomatic code, and the runtime removes costs it can prove unnecessary.

Still, the runtime cannot repair every shelf you build. It cannot make a mutated dictionary key stable. It cannot turn every copy into a view after you have required separate storage. It cannot make cold startup timing equal warmed steady-state timing. Your job is to give the runtime honest contracts and sensible shapes.

Measure warmed code.

Story or Scenario

A small payments team had a nightly reconciliation job that usually finished before anyone arrived in the morning. After a new partner feed launched, the job began running into business hours. The team first blamed the database, then the network, then the new data volume.

A developer traced the hot section and found two shelf problems. Each partner record built several growing lists without any starting capacity, even though the approximate item counts were already known from the feed header. Worse, the job copied slices of arrays into temporary arrays just to inspect small ranges of fields. Those copies became thousands of short-lived shelves.

The team changed the list creation to prepare enough room for the expected books, but not enough to waste large unused shelves. Then they replaced temporary slice copies with span windows where the data only needed immediate inspection. They also found one dictionary keyed by a mutable reference-type object and replaced the key with a stable value whose equality facts never changed after insertion.

No single change sounded heroic. The job became faster because the team stopped rearranging shelves when it only needed to look through windows.

Common Misconceptions

- A list is slow because it can grow. This belief is tempting because growth involves allocation and copying. The correct understanding is that lists are efficient when their growth pattern fits the job. Avoid relapse by asking whether expansion happens rarely, predictably, or inside a hot path.
- Capacity changes what a list means. This is wrong because capacity is storage room, not item count. The list's meaningful contents are the items actually present. Treat capacity as shelf planning, and do not reserve excessive unused room without a reason.
- A dictionary uses only GetHashCode to find a key. This is tempting because hash-based collections talk so much about hashes. The correct model is two-step lookup: GetHashCode finds the shelf label, and

Equals confirms the exact key. Remember that collisions are normal and must remain correct.

- Mutating a dictionary key is safe if the object is still the same object. This confuses object identity with dictionary filing behavior. If changed fields affect GetHashCode, lookup goes to the wrong label. If changed fields affect Equals, lookup can fail during final confirmation. Use immutable keys or avoid changing equality-participating fields after insertion.
- Span of T is a small array. This is wrong because a span owns no storage. It is a stack-only window over existing contiguous memory. Avoid the mistake by asking whether books were copied or only viewed through a start and length.
- ReadOnlySpan of T makes the underlying data permanently immutable. The read-only rule applies through that window. Other valid references to the same storage can still mutate it when the underlying storage allows mutation. Treat ReadOnlySpan of T as a promise about this view, not as a freeze on the whole shelf.
- Memory of T is just a slower Span of T. This is wrong because the main difference is lifetime, not a ranking. Span of T is the short-lived stack-only window. Memory of T is the heap-safe representation for view-like relationships that must be stored or carried across await boundaries.
- .NET 10 optimizations mean allocation choices no longer matter. This is wishful thinking. Escape analysis, devirtualization, inlining, and garbage collector improvements remove some costs when the runtime can prove safety. They do not cancel poor collection design, unstable keys, or unnecessary copying.
- A first benchmark run measures only your program logic. This is wrong on normal .NET execution. First runs can include just-in-time compilation and early tiered compilation behavior. Separate cold-start questions from warmed hot-path questions.

Summary

Collections, spans, and performance instincts all come back to the bookshelf. A list is a shelf that can expand, and expansion copies element slots into larger storage. A dictionary is a labeled index that depends on stable GetHashCode and Equals behavior. A span is a cardboard window over existing contiguous books, not a copied shelf. ReadOnlySpan of T limits what the window can do, ReadOnlySpan of char is the natural view for string data, and Memory of T gives you a heap-safe counterpart when the view must live longer.

Modern .NET helps more than older runtimes did, especially in .NET 10, but the best results still come from clear contracts and honest shapes. Prepare shelves when growth is predictable, without reserving wasteful space. Keep dictionary keys stable. Use windows when you only need an immediate view, and copy when you need ownership or a snapshot. Warm up code before judging hot-path performance. The runtime is an excellent assistant, not a substitute for judgment.

Key Terms

- Capacity: The amount of storage a collection has prepared before it must grow. For a list, capacity is shelf room, not the number of meaningful items currently stored, and excessive unused capacity is still memory you reserved.
- Size: The number of items currently present in a collection. Size is the books actually on the shelf.
- Collection growth: The process of acquiring larger internal storage when a collection runs out of room. Growth often requires allocation and copying of element slots, which means copying values for value-type elements and copying links for reference-type elements, not moving the referenced objects themselves.
- Hot path: A frequently repeated execution route where small costs matter because they happen many times. In this chapter, repeated collection growth and copying are common hot-path costs.
- Dictionary lookup: The process a dictionary uses to find a value by key. GetHashCode chooses the shelf label, then Equals confirms the exact key.
- Hash collision: A normal situation where different keys receive the same hash-based shelf label. A correct dictionary still works because Equals performs the final match.

- Stable key: A dictionary key whose equality and hash-code behavior do not change while it is stored in the dictionary. If the hash code changes, lookup can search the wrong shelf; if equality changes, lookup can fail to recognize the key even when it reaches the right shelf.
- Contiguous memory: Storage where items sit next to one another in one continuous run. Arrays, strings, and slices of array-like storage are common places where this layout matters.
- Span of T: A stack-only window over mutable contiguous memory. It views existing storage through a start and a length instead of owning or copying the data, and its lifetime is limited to the current stack-only scope.
- ReadOnlySpan of T: A read-only stack-only window over contiguous memory. It prevents mutation through that view, but it does not make the underlying storage deeply or permanently immutable; string data is commonly viewed as ReadOnlySpan of char.
- Memory of T: A heap-safe counterpart to Span of T for view-like access that must be stored, passed around more freely, or used across asynchronous boundaries. Use it when the window has to survive beyond the immediate stack-only moment.
- First-class span conversions: A C# 14 feature that makes array-to-span conversions part of the language's regular conversion model. It reduces friction when creating span views, but it does not change what a span is or how long it may live.
- Escape analysis: A runtime proof that an object does not outlive a method. In .NET 10, this can let some objects avoid managed heap allocation, and you do not request it directly.
- Interface call: A call made through an interface contract rather than directly through a known concrete type. Interface calls can be less direct unless the runtime proves the actual target.
- Devirtualization: A runtime optimization that replaces an indirect interface or virtual call with a direct call when the concrete target is known.
- Inlining: A runtime optimization that folds a small called operation into its caller so the call overhead and surrounding work can be optimized together.

- Arm64 garbage collection pause: A pause caused by the garbage collector while running on Arm64 processors. .NET 10 improved these pauses automatically, especially for some collection work.

Mini Quiz

1. **A teaching list starts with enough room for four items. You add a fifth item. What usually happens internally?**

   A. The list changes into a dictionary

   B. The list acquires larger storage and copies existing element slots

   C. The fifth item is rejected until capacity is manually changed

   D. The garbage collector immediately promotes the list to Generation 2

2. **Why does preparing list capacity help when the final size is predictable?**

   A. It changes the equality behavior of the list

   B. It prevents all garbage collection in the application

   C. It can avoid repeated internal expansion and copying

   D. It makes every item immutable

3. **A mutable reference-type dictionary key is inserted, then a field used by its GetHashCode and Equals behavior is changed. What is the best mental model for the failure that can follow?**

   A. The dictionary forgot the value during garbage collection

   B. The key was filed under one shelf label, but lookup may search another or fail the final match

   C. The dictionary refuses all mutable reference types

   D. The runtime changed the object's identity

4. **When is copying the better choice instead of using a span view?**

   A. When the selected data must live independently after the original storage can change or disappear

   B. When you want the garbage collector to ignore all objects

   C. When the view is read-only for a few immediate operations

   D. When the data already sits in one continuous run

5. **When should Memory of T be preferred over Span of T?**

   A. When the view must be stored or survive beyond the immediate stack-only scope, including across an await boundary

B. When you need dictionary lookup by key

C. When you want to force a Generation 0 collection

D. When you want every read to allocate a new array

6. **What is the right lesson from .NET 10 runtime optimizations such as escape analysis, devirtualization, and inlining?**

   A. Allocation choices no longer matter

   B. Mutating dictionary keys is now safe

   C. Clear idiomatic code can become cheaper when the runtime proves it safe

   D. First-run timings now always equal warmed steady-state timings

Answers are provided in the Answer Key at the end of the book.

Reflection Prompts

- Identify a place where you build a list repeatedly and already know the approximate number of items.
- Describe a case where capacity planning would help, then name what excessive unused capacity would cost.
- Describe a dictionary key type you have used, and decide whether its equality facts or hash-code facts can change after insertion.
- Compare a recent data-slicing task with the bookshelf model: did you need an independent copy, or did you only need a temporary window?

Next Steps

Recap of skills gained

You now have a working mental model for how C# code becomes a running .NET program. You can reason from source code to compiler output, from Intermediate Language to just-in-time compiled machine code, and from object allocation to garbage collection.

You have also practiced the key distinctions that shape everyday C# decisions:

- Value semantics versus reference semantics
- Object identity versus value-based equality
- Generic type safety and runtime generic behavior
- Delegates, closures, events, and captured state
- LINQ as deferred work rather than immediate work
- `async` and `await` as compiler-built state machines
- Nullable reference types as compile-time guidance
- Collections, spans, allocations, and performance tradeoffs

The main skill is not memorizing syntax. It is learning to ask, "What does the compiler promise, and what does the runtime actually have to do?"

Recommended next projects

Build small projects that force these ideas into practice:

1. **Allocation journal**

Write a console app that processes text in several ways. Compare string concatenation, `StringBuilder`, spans, and collection growth. Track allocations with profiling tools.

2. **Equality lab**

Create several types that represent the same domain concept as a class, struct, record, and record struct. Test equality, dictionary keys, mutation, and hash behavior.

3. **Deferred execution demo**

Build a LINQ pipeline over an in-memory collection. Add logging inside predicates and selectors so you can hear or see exactly when work happens.

4. **Async service simulator**

Write a program that simulates file reads, web calls, retries, cancellation, and exceptions. Focus on how errors travel through `await`.

5. **Mini event system**

Create a publisher and multiple subscribers. Add lambdas that capture variables, then inspect how changing captured state affects later event calls.

Suggested advanced topics to learn next

After the concepts in this book feel natural, move into areas where the same models keep paying off:

- Benchmarking with BenchmarkDotNet
- Profiling allocations, CPU time, and garbage collection pauses
- Source generators and Roslyn analyzers
- `unsafe` code, pointers, and interop boundaries
- Channels, pipelines, and producer-consumer designs
- Advanced async patterns, cancellation, and backpressure
- ASP.NET Core request processing internals
- NativeAOT tradeoffs for application startup and deployment
- Runtime configuration, diagnostics, tracing, and counters

Treat each topic as an extension of the same core question: what work is being created, where does it live, and when does it run?

How to stay current (docs, release notes, community resources)

Use primary sources first:

- Read the official C# language documentation on Microsoft Learn.

- Track .NET release notes for runtime, library, and SDK changes.
- Follow the .NET Blog, especially performance and runtime posts.
- Review C# language design notes when new language features appear.
- Keep an eye on GitHub discussions in the dotnet/runtime and dotnet/csharplang repositories.

For community learning, choose resources that explain tradeoffs, show measurements, and correct older guidance when the runtime improves. Revisit your mental models with each new .NET release, then test assumptions with small experiments.

Part V: Review Questions

Answer Key

Chapter 1: Thinking Like the Runtime

1. B
2. A
3. C
4. B
5. D
6. C

Chapter 2: From Source to Running Program

1. B. Intermediate Language inside an assembly
2. A. The Common Language Runtime translates that method into native machine code
3. A. The runtime can reuse the translated native code
4. C. The runtime may have translated and later optimized a hot path
5. B. Real behavior observed while the program runs, such as common branches and call targets
6. D. It moves native compilation ahead of program execution after the Intermediate Language assembly stage

Chapter 3: Values, References, Copies, and Text

1. B. The first variable stays unchanged because the second variable received a copy.
2. B. The reference was copied, and both variables can now reach the same object.
3. C. The copied value from the moment boxing occurred.
4. A. The original struct can observe the edited label because the link was copied.
5. A. The changed element, because the array itself is a shared object.

6. C. Reason from copy semantics and reference semantics before thinking about storage.

Chapter 4: Garbage Collection, Object Lifetimes, and Cleanup

1. C. Whether any live path can still reach the object
2. A. They become eligible for collection
3. B. It keeps references to objects that would otherwise become unreachable
4. B. It releases non-memory resources at a chosen time
5. C. The object remains alive because a live path still reaches it
6. A. The subscriber can remain alive because the publisher still has a reference path to it

Chapter 5: Types, Records, Equality, and Operators

1. B. They are not equal because they are different objects
2. D. A record or record struct
3. C. Equal instances must produce matching hash codes for hash-based lookup to work correctly
4. A. The enum can still hold an unnamed underlying value unless validation prevents it
5. B. Construction behavior to be split across parts of one partial type
6. D. The type has two conflicting rulebooks

Chapter 6: Generics as Real Runtime Types

1. B. Constructed generic types exist as real type rulebooks at runtime
2. B. The integer elements are stored in that specific generic list without boxing
3. C. An eligibility rule that limits which case categories can fill a blank slot

4. A. Generic interface
5. D. Because the provider only gives values out, and every archived customer file is also a general customer file
6. A. Naming the generic template rulebook without filling its type slots

Chapter 7: Delegates, Closures, and Events

1. D. A delegate is a type-safe route to callable behavior.
2. B. A closure carries the captured variable slot, not a frozen value.
3. C. They report three, three, and three because they share the same captured counter slot.
4. A. A long-lived publisher can keep a subscriber reachable through its event delegate list.
5. B. Creating a lambda prepares callable behavior, while invoking it runs the behavior.
6. D. Delegate variance follows safe producer and consumer direction when the delegate type allows it.

Chapter 8: LINQ and Deferred Execution

1. B. The new item appears because the query reads the source when enumerated
2. C. It cooks now and stores the result as a stable snapshot
3. A. Deferred LINQ normally repeats the work each time it is enumerated
4. B. In-memory LINQ uses delegates over objects, while queryable LINQ builds expression trees for a provider
5. D. The current value in the captured variable slot when the query runs
6. A. The later filter is now running locally in the application

Chapter 9: Async, Await, and Time

1. C. The pager promising future completion
2. D. It records a continuation and returns control

3. C. The logical method continued, but physical thread identity was not guaranteed
4. B. The continuation may need the captured user interface thread that is blocked
5. A. Async frees a thread during waiting; parallelism uses multiple workers at the same time
6. C. It prevents a thread from being wasted during the wait

Chapter 10: When Things Go Wrong: Exceptions and Failure Design

1. C. A kitchen alarm that interrupts service
2. B. Return an outcome that says the name is unavailable
3. C. The runtime leaves methods outward through the call chain while searching for a handler
4. A. A guard clause should reject the contract violation early
5. A. At the point where the Task is awaited
6. B. The handler silenced the alarm without handling the failure

Chapter 11: Nullability, Patterns, and C# 14 Ergonomics

1. D. Ticket notes that help Roslyn spot risky routes before execution
2. B. Add runtime guards for values required by the contract
3. A. It tests observed shape and can narrow type and null-state after success
4. A. It evaluates the target as missing and skips the assignment
5. B. To name the compiler-generated backing field inside the accessor
6. A. They add an external member-like surface around an existing type

Chapter 12: Collections, Spans, and Performance Instincts

1. B. The list acquires larger storage and copies existing element slots
2. C. It can avoid repeated internal expansion and copying
3. B. The key was filed under one shelf label, but lookup may search another or fail the final match
4. A. When the selected data must live independently after the original storage can change or disappear
5. A. When the view must be stored or survive beyond the immediate stack-only scope, including across an await boundary
6. C. Clear idiomatic code can become cheaper when the runtime proves it safe

Thank You for Reading

We hope this book has been a valuable resource in your learning journey.

Join the unQbd Community

You just built a working mental model of how C# becomes a running .NET program, from IL and JIT to allocations, GC, async, LINQ, and nullability. Now imagine turning that insight into measured performance, cleaner architecture, and deeper .NET diagnostics with the rest of the unQbd library.

Visit unqbd.com/app to start your 7-day Premium trial, then $9.99 per year.

Every book. Every audiobook. $9.99 for the entire year.

Prefer to explore first?

Create a free account at **unqbd.com/register/free** to access curated books, community reviews, and weekly free releases.

If this book helped you, a quick review on Amazon helps other readers find it. Thank you.

www.ingramcontent.com/pod-product-compliance
Lightning Source LLC
LaVergne TN
LVHW060037210926
848481LV00013B/3883